J.R. CLYNES

A Political Life

J.R. CLYNES

A Political Life

Tony Judge

ALPHA HOUSE BOOKS

ALPHA HOUSE BOOKS
London, England
alphahouse7@gmail.com
copyright@2015 Tony Judge
All Rights Reserved
ISBN: 9781518761980

Contents

Acknowledgements

I would like to thank the staff at the British Library, the British Library of Economic and Political Science LSE, and the Library of Nuffield College Oxford for all their friendly help.

Illustrations

1
Introduction

J. R. Clynes was an important figure in the early Labour Party. A founder member of the ILP and the Labour Party, a member of the wartime coalition government of Lloyd George, briefly leader of the Labour Party in 1922, a cabinet minister in both the inter-war minority Labour governments, President of what became the General and Municipal Workers Union for twenty-five years, a member of the Labour Party National Executive Council for thirty-five years, and a Labour MP for thirty-seven years until 1945. This amazingly long career placed him at the heart of the early history of trade unionism and the Labour Party, influential in setting up many of its representative structures, and a key point of liaison between the trade unions and the Party.

Despite this, Clynes has been dismissed by some as a 'nearly man' who failed to defeat MacDonald for the leadership in 1922, and as one of those 'tainted' by close association with the latter in the disastrous 1931 economic and political crisis which plunged the Labour Party into the wilderness. By others, he has been seen as the 'best' leader Labour never had or more recently, in counter-factual speculation, as one of the best prime ministers the country never had.[1]

A part of the explanation for Clynes's neglect may be that, unlike some of his colleagues in the early years of the Labour movement, he left no personal papers of any substance. His colleague Philip Snowden, another important figure in Labour's early history, also left few papers and has suffered a similar biographical neglect. Clynes did publish two volumes of selective memories, self-justificatory in the general way of political memoirs, but a useful source of information on his early life and struggles, and early life as a trade union organiser and Labour politician. They were published in 1937, when he had already assumed the role of an elder statesman in the Labour Party. But was still an MP, and did not want to write anything that might embarrass the Party as it tried to recover from the catastrophe of 1931. But they give a flavour of what it was like serving in the final days of MacDonald's cabinet, with hapless ministers engulfed by the economic and political crisis. Clynes did not try to hide the utter shock and disbelief amongst his colleagues, as MacDonald calmly walked away from the Labour Party he had helped to create and into a coalition dominated by the Tories.

Clynes experienced considerable criticism in his own lifetime, even before 1931, and has continued to be the object of disdain by some on the left ever since. There was his 'pro-war' stance in 1917, seen by some as being excessively patriotic, and the alacrity with which he was willing to serve in Lloyd George's coalition government. This led to such an enthusiasm for coalition government that he wanted it to continue, even after the hostilities had ceased in 1918. There is also his inclusion in a group of Labour leaders accused of over-eagerness to move in aristocratic and royal circles in the 1920's, victims of the so-called 'aristocratic embrace' alleged to have diverted and weakened their socialist resolve. Finally there was his role in the 1929-31 Labour cabinet, supporting Philip Snowden's futile fiscal orthodoxy of a balanced budget while unemployment relentlessly rose.

I have attempted to address these charges and while not entirely rejecting them, arrive at a balanced view of Clynes by setting them in the context of his whole career, seeing him more as a product of his time. Perhaps this allows us to view him in a more sympathetic light, as a practical politician who attempted to keep the Labour Party in play during tumultuous events, and at the same time doing what he could to protect and advance the material conditions of the working class.

His caution and willingness to compromise also left him open to some criticism, and even among his contemporaries he had a reputation for hesitancy and procrastination. These traits partly derive from Clynes's personality, and also from his pioneering work as a trade union organiser for the Gas Workers Union, first in the North-West and then on the national stage. The creation of a new mass-membership union involved getting it accepted by employers, and then persuading them to accept negotiations on wages and conditions at a time when unions were not recognised, and also extremely weak.

Clynes was to form a remarkable partnership with Will Thorne in the Gas Workers Union, that eventually became the GMWU. Thorne was a tough-talking orator, with Clynes as a less dramatic, quietly spoken, patient, and more rational organiser. Clynes and Thorne saw the creation of the Labour Party as an extension of their work to promote the interests of organised labour, a political arm of the labour movement. They were among those who helped to build up the party in the years before 1918, and after the war, replacing the Liberals as the main opposition Party. Finally, power was achieved in 1923 albeit in a minority government. It was a remarkable journey and exciting political time, a crusading mission to create a mass democratic socialist party with sufficient appeal to win elections.

Clynes saw how state power could be harnessed for the greater good of all the people during the First World War. In the Ministry of Food he saw how state resources could be organised and allocated for the benefit of the majority of people, controlling the malign effects in the market such as shortages and profiteering. He never lost this belief in the benign power of the state to plan, organise and provide for the public good, and remained a firm believer in state intervention in the market and control over basic industries.

It is doubtful whether all his colleagues in the Labour cabinet of 1929-31 had such a deep attachment, but the ease with which MacDonald, Snowden and Thomas reneged on what he thought had been shared objectives, shocked Clynes to the core. He refused to join them in the National Government, although he would almost certainly have been given a cabinet post had he done so. Always loyal to the labour movement, after his election defeat in 1931 he returned to union work.

By 1935, when re-elected as an MP, he was one of the older generation in the party and remained an MP on the back benches until 1945. He lived long enough to see so many of his longed for hopes finally achieved by Attlee's Labour government.

Clynes was a patriotic ethical socialist, uninterested in ideology or internationalism, and deeply suspicious of communism or of any political ideas not rooted in the English experience. He had read William Morris and Robert Blatchford, but it is doubtful whether he had ever looked at Marx, and his idealistic socialism was always tempered by what he saw as possible and achievable, the aim always to improve the well-being of working class people. Never one to get trapped in an entrenched point of view Clynes, with his reasonable and emollient approach, was invariably the one put up at conferences to defuse difficult situations, or called upon when union negotiations were deadlocked. His pragmatism, and good judgement, knowing when to be firm and when to compromise, was the key to his success as a trade union negotiator. This was accompanied by a disdain for what he saw as the futility of rhetorical gestures and strident speeches, to which many of his early socialist colleagues were prone.

Clynes was proud of the social class from which he came, and of being one of the first people of manual working class origin to reach a high political office. But he never played up to this, or felt the need to use it for 'political advantage.' This was partly because almost all the first Labour MPs were from the same kind of working class background, and also Clynes was diffident by nature and would have seen it as hypocritical posturing. In his later career, when meeting or attending functions with royalty, he felt it was as a representative of the working class. He saw the working class as part of the nation and fully entitled to be included in all and every official occasion, with the Labour Party best placed to represent them. In 1937 he wrote:

> Labour serves the British people because it is a movement of the people. We have faced the people's problems ourselves, in our own homes and in the humble homes of our parents. Many of us have found, in political life, not a splendid career but an expression of our religion. A position not be viewed as a job but as a Cause.2

But he was also clear that the Labour Party had to govern on behalf of all sections of society, not merely to protect the interests of one section, however large that group might be. However, because the material gap between the working class and other social classes was so wide, there was a great deal of catching up to do and priority would have to be given to the former until there was more equality. The working class were 'in need of first-aid, that is the poorest and most downtrodden. Labour must act as the political Red Cross to those sections of suffering humanity.'2

Clynes shared the simple instinctive patriotism, and popular monarchism of many working class people of the period. This has been seen by some as part of the 'conservatism' of traditional working class communities, an instinctive patriotism born of imperial expansion and royal ceremony. Such spectacle understandably played more of a role in people's lives at a time of mass illiteracy, and was later reinforced by the rapidly expanding popular press from the end of the nineteenth century. Clynes never lost his staunch belief in constitutional monarchy, and periods in ministerial office only served to confirm it. He came to have great respect for George V, particularly for what he regarded as the King's sagacious acceptance of the political and social changes of his time. But his admiration for the monarchy was tempered by the proviso that the occupant of the throne should clearly understand the limitations of their constitutional role, and be prepared to act as a focus for the unity of the people in a politically neutral way. In other respects, he saw through the absurdities of court life, formal dress or ceremonials and so on, most of which he regarded as inconvenient nonsense.

Unlike some of his Labour colleagues he never attended aristocratic soirees, became close to members of the aristocracy, or hobnobbed with society hostesses. Nor did he have any time for titles or the hereditary principle, believing that they made social class divisions deeper and the achievement of a fairer and equable society more difficult. He never had, nor did he seek, any state honours himself, and approved of those who declined them, remaining a backbench MP until 1945. Clyne's patriotism and support for the Empire did not extend to colonial wars or foreign adventures.

Although not a pacifist, like most of his ILP colleagues, he opposed the war in Europe until the last moment in 1918. But with war inevitable he was now in favour' to defeat Germany and arrive at a peace settlement as soon as possible. This issue brought him into conflict with many ILP colleagues, such as the Labour Party leader Ramsay MacDonald. After war was declared, Clynes was proud of the way so many young men from the industrial working classes flocked to volunteer, and spoke enthusiastically at recruitment rallies all over the country. But he supported Labours opposition to conscription, not out of conscientious objection but from a desire to protect the interests of working class families on the Home Front, and to mitigate the effects of the conflict on their domestic lives. He felt he could do this best by exercising influence on the government as an insider, and this partly explains his willingness to serve in the government of Lloyd George, something for which he was criticized both within the Party and outside it.

Clynes was committed to achieving a socialist society, and believed this was possible by parliamentary means in the longer term, while in the meantime compromise and pragmatism were often necessary to exercise influence. The 'all or nothing' approach to achieving socialism involving revolutionary change he thought futile and likely to lead to chaos, tyranny, and suffering for the those it was meant to benefit. It was better to make gradual progress towards a socialist society, however small and hesitant these incremental steps might be, that could provide the basis or larger advances in the future.

In the meantime, planning for that future should be the priority, collecting data, evaluating alternatives, and getting on with the huge task of convincing the people about the benefits of democratic socialism at the grassroots level.

A criticism of this approach is that it was excessively timid and cautious, and allowed the momentum of change to be put back by regressive actions that not only undid past achievements, but were difficult to reverse. Clynes has been accused of failing to oppose MacDonald and Snowden until it was too late in 1931 over the spending cuts. But he was not alone in this, with most of his cabinet colleagues and Labour MP's appearing to be mesmerised by MacDonald, until it was brutally clear that he no longer had any loyalty left for the Labour Party. It was also relevant that, whatever his failings, as a man and a politician, MacDonald still had enormous stature in the Party, retaining a good deal of respect.

The caution displayed by MacDonald and the Labour Party during the General Strike of 1926, and in the economic crisis of 1929, frustrated many. But he had nonetheless 'won' two general elections and Labour had become the second largest party in the country under his leadership. He had ably steered the party through many crisis even though few, including Clynes, were under any illusions about his vanity and weaknesses. There seemed to be no one of comparable stature to replace him, even if it had been possible to defeat him. Clynes stood against him for the leadership in 1922 and been narrowly defeated, ironically mainly through the votes of the 'Red Clydesider's group of ILP members who were to be the bitterest critics of MacDonald in the Party after 1926.

Clynes opposed the 1926 General Strike, although once it began he supported the miners, both personally and though his trade union which had members who were surface workers on strike. He did his best to conciliate between the mine owners, the miner's union and the government but the ultimate defeat was bitter, leaving him and other members of the Labour Party vulnerable to criticism for not giving open support to the strikers.

Despite this, an important key to understanding Clynes's political career was his background as a trade unionist. His socialism was based on working class unity and co-operation, exemplified in the 'New Unionism' of which he was pioneer. He always believed in 'strength through unity' to make trade unionism effective, and this applied to the labour movement as a whole. The Labour Party was founded to be the political organ of a mass working class movement, and not merely as a semi-independent adjunct of the trade unions. Without the trade unions it would not have come into being, and Clynes believed that without their full support and involvement it would not be successful. The prospect of a socialist society would recede even further into the future if disunity and division was allowed to fester. And just as the trade unions continually recruited and educated its members, so the Labour Party should do the same, in order to create a mass Party to spread the gospel of socialism. This had to be a permanent effort, involving education, persuasion and mobilisation through the grassroots, and involving the trade unions, the trades councils, adult education, evening classes, and the local Labour Party branch activities.

If the Labour Party neglected the people and made unwarranted assumptions about their loyalty, then the prospect of Labour governments with sizeable overall majorities was extremely unlikely, given the power of the opposing forces including unscrupulous right-wing newspapers. Although he was defeated in the 1931 Labour electoral collapse, Clynes returned to Parliament in 1935 and remained an MP until 1945 when he retired at 76. He was by then one of the few surviving pioneers of the founding of the ILP and Labour Party, one of the few who had lived long enough to see the election of a Labour Government with a large majority and a mandate for socialist changes. These included policies for which he had worked so long, including the nationalisation of basic industry, and the creation of a welfare state that provided a decent life for all the people.

But despite this, Clynes did not live long enough to benefit personally from the welfare state he had fought for, and just before he died found himself in financial hardship. It was a bitter irony that a man who had spent almost his whole life campaigning for job and income security, pensions and health care was unable to enjoy a poverty free old age. He predeceased his wife and died in 1947, just before any of the welfare state legislation he had waited so long was of benefit to himself.

2
Young Piecer Clynes

John Robert Clynes was born on the 27 March 1869 in Oldham, one of seven children in an Irish immigrant family who had settled in the Lancashire cotton mill town. His father, Patrick, had been a tenant farmer in Ireland who had been forced to join the wave of departures following the potato blight and famine of 1851. The incomes of tenant farmers dried up, they were unable to pay the rent, and were soon evicted from their smallholdings. Patrick was one of thousands facing destitution who emigrated, either by taking the long sea voyage to America and Australia or by crossing the Irish Sea to England.

By the middle of the nineteenth century Oldham was one of the most productive of all the Lancashire cotton towns, well on the way to becoming the most prolific, making it the cotton spinning capital of the world. The spinning of cotton was introduced in 1778, many mills were established and urbanisation was rapid. By 1818 there were eighteen mills in the town employing thousands of men, women and children, and the population grew steadily over the the next hundred years from 12,000 in 1801 to 137,000 by 1901.[1]

At the time Patrick Clynes arrived over 30% of the population in Oldham were employed in cotton textiles, and there was considerable resentment about the new arrivals most of whom were from Ireland, and a rising fear that they would undercut wages and steal their jobs, with the anti-Irish feeling being compounded by both ignorance and superstition. Trying to settle and integrate was not easy for the new arrivals, and they had to cluster where they could in some of the worst slum housing in the town. The earlier growth in textile manufacturing, railway and canal construction was over, and jobs were getting more difficult to obtain. After he had worked for some time as a machine-minder in a textile mill, Patrick was made redundant and glad enough to get another job with Oldham Corporation, as a grave-digger in the cemetery and general labourer in the municipal parks.

The 'cotton famine' caused by the American Civil War led to a slump in the Lancashire cotton industry, with many workers made unemployed. Then when supplies of raw cotton resumed, the textile industry recovered and Oldham was soon overtaking Manchester and Bolton in the construction of new mills, as this second phase of expansion began. The boom continued throughout the 1870s, and the industry produced vast wealth for its owners and investors.

For the workers, however, toiling in these mills it continued to provide only a minimal income, with a standard of living barely above subsistence level. There was constant threat of unemployment due to the regular fluctuations in the demand for cotton cloth, and almost total dependence on the whims of overseers, managers, and owners. The other non-skilled jobs available in textile towns like Oldham paid little better, or even worse, and it was difficult to escape from the insecurity and awful working conditions in the mills.

Whatever work people did in the town, it was not possible to escape the constant smoke belching out from the array of chimneys, casting a grey pall over the town from morning until night. Although Patrick Clynes may escaped the from mill life, he still had to work a ten-hour day for the paltry sum of £1 a week, which never rose above £1/5s in twenty-five years.

The work extended beyond grave digging to other types of general labouring in the local parks, working out in the open in all weathers. He never enjoyed sick pay or paid holidays, and any time taken off for illness led to wages being stopped until he returned to work. And hanging over him, as for so many others at the time, was the ever-present threat of the kind of penury which led the workhouse. The walls of these places loomed in the in the background, a menacing presence as a place for for the destitute.

John Clynes remembered his father as a quiet, kind, and rather grave man who had a sensitive understanding of human behaviour. He was generally mild in temperament, a loving father and husband who could offer little else to his family as his life was a continual struggle of manual labour and poverty. He did not drink, unusual among the labouring classes at the time, and passed on his innate kindness and consideration for others to his children. The little education available for them cost him one penny a week for each, a considerable sacrifice with six children.

As the family grew, Patrick's income was barely adequate to feed and clothe them. Their diet was basic, typical of the working poor of the time, and made up largely of bread, dripping, potatoes, a few other vegetables and tea. It was extremely rare to eat meat or fish, and the resulting lack of protein affected health and physical development, with diseases related to poor diet rife such as rickets. The Clynes family were fortunate in managing to avoid such disasters for without medical attention such diseases were often fatal.

The family housing were extremely poor, typical of that available for the unskilled working class in all the mill towns of Lancashire, as well as the nearby metropolis of Manchester. Their homes consisted of row upon row of two-up two-down 'cottages', three or four storied terraces, or equally ramshackle dwellings huddled around courtyards or 'courts'. All of these became slums soon after being hastily put up to house the mill workers, and by the 1860's their condition was even worse.

These hovels still lacked running water or sanitation, were usually overcrowded and plagued with damp, cold with a smoky atmosphere inside and out. There was a lack of adequate ventilation from the coal fires which were the only means of warmth, and outside the chimney stacks belched out smoke all over the town. The effect on the health of the people huddled together in these communities was disastrous, and exacerbated the rate of both adult and infant mortality. Although the young John Clyne's and his siblings seem to have been fairly robust and healthy, they were fortunate to survive childhood and early death from rickets, diphtheria or pneumonia.

In 1874 at the age of five, Clyne's began attending the local Board School where basic instruction was provided in reading, writing and arithmetic, together with some bible study. He disliked the school intensely, bored by the narrow curriculum, regimented teaching methods, and the corporal punishment of which he received his share. Although children could remain in full-time education by this time up to the age of thirteen, it was possible for parents to withdraw them from the age of ten to work on a part-time basis. Clynes could not wait to leave early, and his parents would have welcomed any extra wages he could bring in to supplement the household budget.

He was a small child for his age, and rather thin, who had no ambitions beyond leaving school and going to work half-time in a mill. He went to the Dowry cotton textile mill as a 'junior piecer', working in the mornings while continuing to attend school in the afternoon. The mill was located in Turner Street, one of over sixty mills in Oldham at this time.2 The 'little piecer' worked from six in the morning until noon. For these six hours work the pay was half a crown, and involved running between the spinning machines, removing broken cotton threads which had broken off from the ends of the spindles. It required speed of foot and considerable dexterity, darting between and underneath the swinging arms of the spindles.

Children were employed at this because of their smallness and dexterity, but the work could be extremely dangerous with the chance of being caught by one of the flying spindles. If this happened it could lead to serious injury or even death, with no protection of any kind. The ten year old boy could not even wear shoes or clogs for fear of slipping on the oily wooden floor. At the end of shift his feet would invariably be bloodied from splinters in the floor. This hard and dangerous work took place amid the noise of the clattering machines, and in a murky atmosphere of gas light that was the only illumination. The boy longed for the dinner break that came at noon, when he was free to walk the two miles home for the afternoon school session.3

The experience of work suddenly made the school lessons seem less boring, in fact a relief after the arduous labour of the mornings. He began to take a closer interest in his lessons, but Clynes was one of those children who resist rote-learning and memorising large chunks of undigested information, to reproduce it on demand. Even at that young age he preferred to read and think for himself, deciding what was interesting and useful to know. In this way he had the time to think about what he read, making sure he understood it well before picking up another book. This method of self-learning suited him better than the narrow curriculum and instruction at school which never motivated him or inspired his imagination, apart from some Shakespeare and poetry. He could make poetry come alive by it turning it into mental pictures for himself, which he later conjured up in his mind on the mill floor during the long hours of drudgery.4

At last, at twelve he could finally leave school and begin working full-time to earn 10 shillings a week. But he had not stopped his own self-education for he was now able to read and write and had basic numeracy, so started what he saw as his real education.The nineteenth century was the age of the autodidact, as self-education became possible for the increased numbers departing from elementary schools with some basic literacy and and numeracy. This at least provided the basis for self-improvement, although self-education was inevitably unsystematic and did not lead to formal qualifications. Most autodidacts came from the skilled working class, and Clynes was more unusual in coming from the ranks of the unskilled working class, those who were always living on the brink of absolute poverty and destitution.

It was a 'real' education in the sense of greater knowledge and understanding for the sake of it, rather than any other reason. In this sense it was 'pure' education unadulterated by the need to pass examinations, winning prizes, or gain employment. Clynes was part of a large number of working class people all over the country who were doing the same, and his personal focus was in English literature and language. In widening his reading, both knowledge and vocabulary were increased, and raised his horizons above the back-streets of Oldham as well as nourishing his imagination.

There were few libraries in Oldham, books were expensive and no cinema or radio. The lack of mobility meant the working class remained largely stuck in their grey environment, ignorant of the outside world. There were no cars, nor were bicycles yet common for travelling far beyond their town or village.There were no paid holidays, with sparse public transport and only a to Manchester city. But there were several second hand bookshops in the backstreets of Oldham, and the books were sold on market stalls. Clynes spent his free time browsing through them, and he came across old and tattered volumes which he could only read with some difficulty and just afford to purchase. These included an old dictionary which cost sixpence that he had saved up for weeks to buy, and which he poured over for many months. He had to read by candlelight in the cramped room that he shared with his brother and sister, for there was no gaslight and even candles cost 3 pennies each.5

During these long hours of candlelight study, Clynes copied out the words and the meanings of those that most interested him, and which he did not already know. He would then look them up in his dictionary and try speaking phonetically the words he had never heard before. The longer the word was, the better and he rolled the syllables and sound over his tongue, savouring the beauty of the language. In this way he built up his vocabulary and knowledge, and was soon able to purchase a copy of *Cobbetts Grammar*. This cost was for him the huge sum of 9 pennies, and used it to try toput the words he had learned into sentence form. But there was a limit to what the young boy could teach himself unaided, and he eventually reached the point where his lack of formal education was a barrier to further learning. This frustration was shared with many other working class children whose abilities and talents were frustrated by their enforced ignorance.

As he grew older Clynes came to realise that enforcing

ignorance was a means of social control, and in order to be liberated from the chains of ignorance the working had to come together in unityto push for reform and to create more opportunities for all. He that education was the key to understanding theinjustices of capitalism, but society, but to also gain equal access to knowledge that which was the right of every individual. For Clynes, and so many others, the effort of self-improvement against all odds was a key to his own political awakening. The connection between reading and this awakening was to crucial and the more literate, who read Dickens, Ruskin, Shakespeare, and Carlyle tended towards socialist view of society while those who read the racing papers tended to continue voting Tory or Liberal. The new tabloid press hoped to attract the literate reader, but were full of trivial distractions of all kinds, and heavily biased towards the Tories. The countering of its influence was to be a major problem for the fledgling labour movement as it started to organize. Many idealists found that knowledge alone was not enough, and the ideas in Shakespeare, Balzac, Morris and Shaw had to be shown to be as relevant.6

The discovery of Shakespeare in particular was a great help to Clynes in becoming more politically aware. He read in *Twelfth Night* 'Be not afraid of greatness' and so encouraged by the Cooperative Society librarian he read through all the plays. He found they included characters such as WatTyler and Jack Cade who seemed like heroes In *Julius Caesar* 'the realisation came to me that it was a mighty political drama' concerned with class-struggle, not 'just an entertainment'. It was a remarkable insight for a twelve year old untutored boy, and showed how literary self-education could arouse a political interest in modern society. The great writers and dramatists were at least accessible if you could at least read, and required no instruction, so it is not surprising that it was a largely literary self-education. Clyne's, and others like him, became familiar with great dramatists like Shakespeare, so that later as adults they would read them regularly and as naturally as any novel and quote large sections of text.7

Then he answered an advertisement from three elderly blind men in the town who were looking for someone to read the newspapers to them. Clyne's went for a trial, and they were sufficiently satisfied to give him the job, gruffly telling him that he would do. So the weekly sessions reading to them from the local Oldham papers started, and he found the task delighted him. He saw it as a performance, doing his best to make the readings more interesting by emphasising syllables and varying the pitch of his voice for emphasis. His listeners would often interrupt, asking him to repeat interesting parts, and clearly enjoying it. In this way Clynes developed an appreciation of the power of spoken words, and some inkling of what could be done with them. He learned their potential for entertaining, informing and affecting the emotions of people.

When he had completed his newspaper reading task, he would sit there listening to the old men discussing the stories they had just heard, arguing about politics and the injustice in the lives of people such as them. This feedback provided the boy with further notions of social justice and equality, and the frustration and anger of people denied both. From there it was a short step for to realise it might be possible to change the current state of things, that they were not fixed in stone for all time but willed by the powers of others.8

Although it would be too simplistic to make a strong connection between the desire for self-improvement and the foundation of a labour movement, it did play a part in spreading knowledge and in encouraging aspiration to political leadership. This raised political awareness, fed into class solidarity and socialist belief. At the same time it could also lead into a more conservative frame of mind, influencing imperial loyalties, cultural snobbery and even working class Torysm.3 It depended on the reading material used in the self-education process, and many of the early socialists were influenced by reading the work of Ruskin, Morris, J.S. Mill, and the Bible, as well as Shakespeare and Milton.

This was true of Clynes who by the age of thirteen was familiar with Renan's *Life of Jesus,* which he claimed helped to give him the strength and courage to question the injustices heaped on the weak in the name of progress. In addition to this private reading, he spent the three pennies a week he was paid by the blind clients on extra tuition from an old schoolmaster who held classes on two nights a week. In these he received more systematic tuition, and was encouraged to widen his reading further. This he continued to do in the reading room of the Oldham Equitable Co-operative Library, by attending free lectures in the town, as well as continuing to search through the second-hand bookstalls.9

The appearance of public libraries, founded either by public subscription or philanthropic donation, became important sources of information and knowledge for the poor in the age before mass literacy. The young Clynes was a regular user, and the sheer delight of having the free access to these wondrous gifts helped to convince him that while education was the key to social progress, ignorance was its enemy. But he still continued to buy the occasional book, and when he was eighteen he spent what was for him the large sum of one shilling on an old copy of John Ruskin's *The Seven Lamps of Architecture.* It enthralled him, as much as for the sound of the language as the content:

> ...the grace and nobility of phrase with which these authors clothed their thoughts, impressed me far more deeply than did the thoughts themselves.... I read and re-read this book, and so illuminating was the love I held for it that, before I had perused it the third time, its every subtlety of meaning was as much my own intimate possession as a young lover's memory of his virgin kiss is his.10

He could afford to purchase only a few books of his own and when he did it was a rare luxury. Instead, most of his reading was done in the Equitable Co-operative Society Library where, sitting at the table, he continued to read Shakespeare, Ruskin, Dickens or whatever other authors he could discover. He could see the political dramas in *Julius Caesar,* and also the links between the state of the working class and industrial capitalism in Dicken's *Hard Times.* But there was little information available about the wider world in working class communities like Oldham at the time, either in popular newspapers or cheap new books. The postal service hardly made any impact with only six deliveries per household a year, one of the lowest rates of delivery in the country which were not unusual in manufacturing areas. Most of the inhabitants rarely travelled more than a few miles away from the town and to them, as Clynes later recalled, "... the rest of the world was a shadowy place merging into the boundaries of unreality"[11]

Within a short time he became a 'senior piecer' at the mill, but was already feeling restless and thinking about how he could improve not only his own conditions but also all of the other workers who laboured so long in the many mills in the town. From the outset he always thought of this problem in terms of communal or cooperative effort, for he realised without unity among the poor nothing much could be achieved of lasting value. He was still small and slight in stature, and his diminutive appearance was accompanied by a rather introspective and shy personality. He did not yet have enough confidence to do much about his convictions for social and political change, but in 1883 he began attending public political meetings.

These were mainly about Irish issues, which were of great interest to the many Irish in the town, and attracted large crowds to listen to nationalist and

Home Rule speakers . There was a large Irish population in other Lancashire towns, and the Irish National League were keen to recruit converts to the cause of Irish home rule. As he listened to a number of speakers arguing the the case for Irish freedom, Clynes was highly impressed by a young Irishman named Byrne, not much older than himself, who also spoke of other things close to his heart such as social reform and working class unity.

It may have been the power of the young Irishman's words or the passion with which he spoke them, but Clynes was impressed with the effect they had on the crowd who loudly cheered. On one occasion Clynes raised an objection to something, but instead of ignoring it Byrne asked him to elaborate the point. But the young man still did not have enough confidence to speak at any length in public, and he shyly declined. But later in conversation Byrne told him he was quite right to interrupt the speech and should make a speech of his own. He also told Clynes that knowledge and reason were not enough whatever your argument, it had to be persuasive to convince an audience.

This was a first lesson in public speaking and one Clynes never forgot, although he was unable become a charismatic orator or simulate emotion as a rhetorical weapon. Instead, he had to work with the grain of his own personality, developing techniques suited to his strengths. His style would always be more natural and conversational, delivered slowly and without emotion but always quiet, reasonable and persistently dogged. Even for one who was not a 'natural' public speaker, it was necessary to learn how to 'project' and to 'work' an audience, particularly as public meetings were the main form of political communication at this time. They attracted some very large crowds and were eagerly anticipated, whether indoors or in the open air spaces. As a form of mass political participation they were often raucus occasions with uninhibited heckling and abuse, sometimes deteriorating into disorder and violence.

The two young friends decided to start their own debating club, and organise debates in an old disused stone quarry just outside the town. These were held in the evenings after work, when most of the workers in the mills could attend. Byrne and Clynes always spoke either for or against the issue, and usually heckled each other mercilessly. In this way, Clynes learnt to think on his feet quickly, and deal with heckling and interruptions. The experience also helped to refine his beliefs about social justice and equality, in particular the rights of the working class to have decent wages, working and living conditions.

It also enabled him, at the young age of fifteen, to develop enough confidence to write letters to the local press on the subject of working life in a mill and on the conditions of work. He signed these letters as *Piecer*, the anonymity being a safer option, as he could easily have been sacked. They contained reasoned arguments for practical improvements in working conditions rather than moral denunciations of the employers. They described the conditions that Clynes was experiencing every working day in the mill, and he knew from first-hand experience the dangers and discomforts of the mill life.12

He had to rise at 4 am in the dark each morning and then, after a meagre breakfast, he started the three mile walk to the mill. There was no more light at the mill when he got there, the only illumination being gas jets which were deliberately kept low. When it came time to trudge home after the long days labour was over, darkness had again fallen with the same low gas light in the streets. In his letters, for which he was becoming more well-known locally, Clynes described the dangerous work machinery, completely unguarded, and the injuries that were suffered daily without any compensation paid to the victims. He also described the suffering of the children who could be heard weeping with exhaustion at the end of a long day, and the employment of young girls and women, an indictment of the unfettered free market capitalism of the times.14

In the increasingly frequent letters to the press, *Piecer* began to advance the notion that rather than trying to persuade the existing political parties to accept reform, it would be more effective for labour to be directly represented by its own party. This was an advanced idea in 1884, and to the authorities a subversive one, for even trade unions were seen as disreputable or even worse.

From the responses he received to his letters in the press, and in conversations with friends and workmates in other mills, Clynes soon learned that opposition to labour reform did not only come from the mill owners. There was also scepticism from some of the mill-workers themselves, an early experience for the fledgling union organiser and politician of working class conservatism. He was unwise to assume all people shared the same idea of what best served their own interests. In the cotton mills it was usually the older spinners who poured scorn on his proposed reforms, including more widespread education on the grounds it would just make the workers discontented and desire what was beyond their attainment. These older workers jealously guarded their senior status, the skilled work that enabled them to enjoy higher wages. Clynes realised that spreading more information about the facts of working life in the textile mills was not enough, but had to be accompanied with education and persuasion. This work should be done by strong labour unions representing all the workers, not various unions represented sectional interests of many different groups of workers, and supported by a political party dedicated to promoting the interests of labour.

Clynes knew his job at the mill always hung by a thread, and he could be sacked at any time. He had to be careful what he said at work and what he was seen reading, and despite the anonymity of his letters to the press his identity could soon be discovered. But he was determined to press ahead, and in 1886 at the age of 17 he was ready to begin organising the piecers into their own union. Their grievances were by now considerable, with a fixed wage for a 12 hour day with no pay for any extra time. Although officially starting work at 6 am, they had to come in early to clean and oil the spinning machines which had to be repeated during the half-hour breakfast break, and dinner breaks. All this extra work was unpaid but compulsory and was the source of much bitterness and constant complaints for it was in reality exploitation on top of their normally exploitative conditions.

There were a growing number of other piecers who shared Clynes' view that this extra work should be paid, and he organised a protest by turning up to work at 6 am instead of half an hour earlier. But when the day came the others lost their courage, leaving only Clynes to get to the mill at 6 am while the other piecers came in early as usual to prepare the machines. He was called in the see the foreman, expecting dismissal, but instead the kindly man showed some sympathy and allowed him back to work, perhaps hoping to gain his goodwill, and allowed him to arrive at the official time in future. The incident was a salutary lesson about always daring to question unchallenged injustices, but to expect difficulty in obtaining the unity needed to make the protest effective. Not only did the hierarchy of occupations and skills in most workplaces mean jealously guarded privileges, but even within a particular trade people were frightened of losing their jobs as a result of industrial action.13

It was only a small personal victory, but it spurred him on to think of widening his campaign for improving conditions. The piecers belonged to the Spinner's Union but were not treated as a separate category of member, and had no separate representation. The leaders of the union were mostly elderly spinners who were mainly concerned only with improving the conditions of the spinners, and there was a general feeling among them that it was no bad thing for the younger piecers to 'go through the mill as their fathers did before they became spinnersthemselves. Until the piecers had a separate representation it was unlikely that their pay and conditions would improve. Clynes had to convince as many as was possible about this, and persuade them to set up their own union. He and few others who thought the same way started trying to organize 'Piecers Union,' but it was an uphill struggle.

Eventually there was enough support for a meeting to be held in Bolton, another important mill town. When it was Clynes' turn to speak, the chairman put his hand on the young man's shoulder and said to the crowd, "This lads, is Piecer Clynes, who writes all the newspaper articles about us!" Up until that point he no idea that the letters had been so widely read or that he was so well known outside of Oldham. This gave him some extra confidence to outline all the arguments for improving pay and working conditions. The meeting ended with a resolution that was approved to form a separate Piecers Union, and Clynes made his way home on the train pleased, but knowing he had to be up early the next morning to clock on for work.15

The difficulties of recruiting piecers to a new union without full-time organizers was soon evident, and Clynes spent all his spare time writing letters, organising meetings and trying to co-ordinate some kind of membership drive in all the Lancashire mill towns. The opposition of the Cotton Spinners Union was always likely to be a major barrier, as they were very reluctant to weaken their own bargaining position by allowing the piecers to leave. They often had a close, sometimes cosy, relationship with the mill-owners who also had self-interest in only dealing with a single union. It was an advantage to the spinners that all the cotton operatives were bound tightly together in a single union, giving more strength and bargaining power. In the 1880s about 90% of all spinners belonged to the union enabling it to control supply of labour and improve pay and conditions for some. They were successful enough, for the working conditions and wages of the cotton spinners better than most other industrial workers in the country.14 Most of the piecers eventually became spinners themselves and moved up the pay scale, so they had some incentive to remain in the spinners union. Another valuable lesson was learned by Clynes, that resolutions and impassioned speeches were one thing but to be effective a union had to be backed up with full-time organization, speak directly to the interests of its members, and have the power to negotiate with employers.

Despite all his difficulties, Clynes became something of a hero in Oldham, among the piecers at least. The secretary of the new union, James Haslam, described Clynes speaking at a meeting in 1888:

> The turn of Clynes came at 9 o'clock. He was nothing to look a frail lad, pale and serious in ungainly clothes. For three quarters of an hour the piecer-orator spoke with well-measured sentences of sincerity and grammatical precision. The audience, which had not been easy to control, laughed with him and was listened to him. Afterwards the chairman of the committee said to me, "Where did you get that lad from? The country will know summat about him – if he lives!"16

It was a brave enterprise, but being young and bold he stifled his natural caution to get the new union off the ground even though it was hard work, and the progress slow.

While he was occupied with the new union, he still found time to meet and court a young girl called Mary Harper, a mill-girl and sister of his friend Thomas Harper. She was quick-witted, very aware politically and interested in the new union. Mary worked in a neighbouring mill, but when she came to work at the Dowery mill she grew closer to Clynes and became his inspiration and encourager, always supporting him in the union activities. He, in turn, found that being in love gave extra meaning to the work he was doing, as it did for her. She had an absolute faith in him as well as in the cause they shared, and soon they were making plans to get married. But he was only seventeen and Mary was even younger, so they had to wait. 17

The year in which the Piecers Union was officially formed was one of considerable industrial and political unrest in the country. The long economic depression that had begun in 1873 had made social conditions even worse, with higher unemployment and lower wages. In February 1886, Clynes read in the newspapers about demonstrations of the unemployed in the East End of London and in Trafalgar Square which created huge national interest. There had been speeches by John Burns and H.M Hyndman, the former carrying a Red Flag, and afterwards the crowd moved off towards Hyde Park. A section broke away and rushed down Pall Mall towards St James's, smashing the windows of the clubs as they went. The main meeting then broke up and marched off down Oxford Street, where they faced a baton charge from the police. In November 1887 there was another great protest meeting on the Irish issue, that many socialists saw as a parallel example of repression of both the Irish and English working class. The march of 10,000 converged into Trafalgar Square led by Annie Besant, John Burns and others who were mainly from the Social Democrat Federation. Bernard Shaw was one of the speakers, and a force of two thousand police officers were deployed. There were serious clashes with the police and militia, and women and children were among the injured with three dying from their injuries, and the next Sunday there were further demonstrations and more violence.

These events were reported with alarm in the Tory and Liberal press, but as the news filtered through to the working class there was a resentment that fed into rising industrial discontent. They created great interest in Oldham among the Irish immigrant population, who followed the aftermath in the press. The closure of Trafalgar Square to political meetings and the imprisonment of John Burns, were seen as part of a pattern of subjugation of the working class. It was natural for many to extend this to include their own insecurity of employment, low wages and appalling working and living conditions. For a time it seemed to be a crucial historical moment which could have led to a variety of outcomes, either of a revolutionary form or in support for radical peaceful change.

The revolutionary socialist SDP had some support in Lancashire but insufficient organization or membership to instil a revolutionary purpose. Worker's increasingly looked to their trade unions to push for the kind of changes they sought, and the more cautious older unionism increasingly came under challenge. The attitude of younger and more militant unionists was expressed forcibly by the speeches and writings of Tom Burns who agreed that trade unions had done a good job in the past, but were now merely concerned with maintaining wage levels. He wrote in 1886 that 'the true unionist policy of aggression seems entirely lost sight of; in fact the average unionist of today is a man with a fossilized intellect, either hopelessly apathetic, or supporting a policy which plays directly into the hands of the capitalist exploiter'.18

At this stage Clynes, despite his natural caution, tended to sympathise with these sentiments, frustrated by the obstruction and 'conservatism' of the moderate Spinners Union. But he thought that the key problem was the lack of a voice for organised labour in Parliament, which was now essential to give a strong political voice to the workers discontents. Although he understood the frustrations that led to militant action, he already had a horror of violence of any kind to which it often led on the picket line, and had never wanted or called for the piecers to go on strike. He did not think that militant industrial action should be part of a wider political struggle, leading to the barricades and street violence, and the concept of a syndicalist 'general strike' was to him unthinkable. His preference was to hold back militant strike action in reserve as an ultimate sanction, but not as a bargaining tactic, and only to use as the last resort. It should always be combined with the political pressure of the labour movement as whole to improve pay and conditions.

3
A 'Sixpenny Cigar'

While exciting political events were taking place in the wider world, Clynes was trying to find a way to leave mill work in order to devote time to full-time union organising. But he also wanted to get married to Mary, and needed enough income to support a home. To leave the mill and work full-time organising the piecers union was an risky option, with no pay and a highly uncertain future. For the time being he had to remain a piecer and do his union work in his spare time, having completed a twelve-hour shift. He was only twenty years old and earning £1 a week, but with the optimism of youth and full of idealism he undertook the burden gladly.

It was a life full of organising, attending meetings and recruiting members, time-consuming work to be done in the evenings and weekends which left him with very little leisure. There was also travelling involved to the other mill towns in Lancashire, which was difficult and expensive, and the fares hard to find. At the often large recruitment meetings, Clynes had to learn to develop a persuasive form of public speaking and develop a thick skin, for although the crowd was generally well disposed to him there were always some present opposed to the new union. They were mostly piecers, but sometimes spinners, in their caps, clogs and mufflers. The meetings could be in a hired hall, or outside the mill-gates or on open ground somewhere, very noisy with a good deal of raucus whistling, shuffling and stamping of feet. After the speeches began it was not long before the hecklers started shouting their interruptions, some of whom were revolutionary socialists who had come to the meeting straight from the pub, usually well-oiled.1

The prospect of a new union alarmed the mill-owners and they were obstructive from the outset, which added to the uphill struggle. The infant union lacked any kind of external support from political parties, newspapers, or the other unions. The police frequently broke up meetings and even arrested the speakers, well aware of the anger of local mill owners at the temerity of their workers protesting about working conditions. The only finance came from the voluntary collections made at the meetings, but this produced little enough apart from an occasional sovereign which a middle class sympathiser might contribute.

But there were enough real grievances to generate support from within the cotton mills for the new union, particularly over the dangerous working conditions. Although factory inspections now took place for safety reasons, and some protection from dangerous machinery was installed, accidents occurred quite frequently. The victims received no compensation for their injuries or for time off work. Nor were there any paid holidays, works canteens to take meals or tea breaks, and no sport or other recreational facilities. In addition, there was no legal security of employment, and the number of hours worked were decided in an arbitrary way by the employer. There was no legal right to strike, and industrial action of any kind could lead to instant dismissal.

As part of his work trying to get the Piecers Union organised, Clynes was also involved in the general promotion of trade union activity in Oldham, and this brought him into contact with the gas workers. The National Union of Gasworkers and General Labourers was a new union, founded in 1889 by Ben Tillett and Will Thorne among others. Thorne, who had recently become the General Secretary, was involved in the 1886 march of unemployed workers to Trafalgar Square. He had been one of the casualties of 'Bloody Sunday,' and something of a hero and well-known figure in trade union circles. Clynes admired him immensely, and when two young men wanted to form a local branch of the NUGGL he agreed to help by acting as the district secretary. Possibly because progress was so slow with his own proposed union, he began organising recruitment meetings for the new branch of the NUGGL instead, and at one meeting Thorne himself came to speak.

A large bluff cockney, full of rhetorical flourishes, Thorne was in many ways the opposite of Clynes in personality. But they got along well, and Thorne was impressed by Clynes' experience and knowledge of workplace conditions and problems in Lancashire. He observed the crowd listening to this diminutive young man, 'a mere slip of a lad, hardly more than a boy. Having come to be amused, I remained to be amazed. About three quarter of an hour's dissertation from this stripling, I decided he knew as much about Lancashire's industrial troubles as I did myself', and so Thorne quickly offered Clynes a job with the union.[2]

The meeting between the two was crucial moment for Clynes's later union and political career. Thorne took him aside, and after quizzing him about his work and experience trying to start his union, offered him a job as Lancashire area organiser for the Gas Workers and General Labourers Union. The young man did not have to think long before accepting the offer. The wages were 30 shillings a week, but he would have to pay his own expenses, and in some ways it seemed another leap in the dark, full of uncertainties and insecurity. And yet it was a way out of the mill and into union organising on a full-time basis, even if it did mean leaving behind the piecers union project. It would also give him the chance to advance the cause of the unskilled workers, who were without organization or protection.3

To go from a mill worker to a full-time union organiser was a tremendous step for the young Clynes, but once he had made up his mind it was an irrevocable one for if the gamble did not come off he would find it almost impossible to obtain employment again in an Oldham mill or anywhere else. But he said his farewells to his mill life with few regrets, and soon he and Mary decided to get married, and rented a cottage in Oldham for a few pounds a week. It was very small, but they managed to furnish it with a few pieces of second hand furniture purchased from their meagre savings. They bought curtains, a chair or a table as they could afford it, and the novelty of married life made it seem a great adventure.

Will Thorne was aware that the success of his new union depended on recruiting talented local people, and he chose district secretaries who were good organisers who could work independently. He liked people who could think for themselves, and were not willing to accept unquestioningly the instructions handed down from head office. The local officials would know conditions intimately on the ground, far better than the headquarters staff could, and could be relied upon to know the best tactics to suit local conditions. The work of a union organiser was as difficult as Thorne warned, but at least there was no rival union this time

The recruitment of new members was also more likely because of the appalling conditions experienced by gas workers. They often worked 12-hour shifts, which could be extended compulsorily to 18 hours by the arbitrary decision of managers. As in the textile industry, the workers were expected to be entirely flexible and work extra hours when required, which usually meant when demand suddenly increased. This was invariably during the winter months, when some weeks the men had to work upwards of 80 hours. But their wages were always low, there was no extra overtime pay, and the work was often hard and dangerous.

When the NUGGL finally negotiated an 8-hour day in the industry, it was a remarkable achievement and recruitment increased even more, soon reaching 20,000. As the North West Regional organiser, covering one of the largest areas in the country, Clynes had a significant role in the national union. He travelled much further away now, which meant going far from Lancashire for the first time in his life, to London on occasion and as far away as Plymouth. On the way to these meetings and

conferences, and as his train travelled on through the
countryside he was impressed not only by the scenery
but by the working people he saw. They included an
array of porters, engine drivers, and occasionally a type of
passenger that caught his eye. He thought of the common
experiences and class interests they shared despite their
different accents, dress and occupations. This gave more
force to his dream that one day they would all be able to
join together in unity, an organised labour movement in
a moral crusade for a better world.3

He was also impressed by the changing scenery of
England, the beauty of the countryside, the houses in
mellow redbrick and stretches of green landscape as far
could be seen. There was none of the soot and dirt of
industrial Lancashire, just the great beauty that existed
outside of the factories and slums, and to which he
knew the workers had no access.

The contrast between the beauty of the natural world
and the virtual imprisonment of working people in
industrial areas, denied access to the free gifts of nature,
filled him with indignation. The many who laboured for
so little so that the few could enjoy leisure, beauty and
culture. This sense of moral outrage, based on a rural-
urban divide, was not unusual among early socialists, and
a common feeling of many of its pioneers that persisted
well after 1918. The countryside and all it had to offer,
unpolluted by capitalist exploitation, was contrasted with
the town and industrial production. The building of a
New Jerusalem in a green and pleasant land underlay the
crusading zeal of early socialists, an almost religious
conviction that they occupied the moral high ground,

and the fight to correct these ills should be fought with a missionary zeal.4

As the regional organiser of the gas workers union in Lancashire, Clynes had very little support with no office or clerical help. He had to undertake all the work alone including speaking over a large region to gas workers, building workers, and others in every town. He also had to distribute handbills in pubs and on street corners, as well as completing the clerical tasks of keeping records of members and collecting subscriptions. The antagonism of the employers continued unabated, and there was the constant danger of being arrested or imprisoned, or labelled an "agitator" by the press. When the lamplighters in Oldham, who were members of the union, went on strike, Clyne's had to organise a system of picketing to prevent the employment of 'blackleg' labour. The employers wrote to the local newspaper alleging the lamplighters had to walk in the gutters, while Clyne's walked along the pavement smoking a sixpenny cigar! In order to disregard such lying absurdities he had to develop a thick skin, a useful early training for the years to come.

The 1890s were a turbulent decade for the 'new' trade unions, representing the largely unskilled and previously non-unionised workers. There were a large number of industrial disputes, and the unions used its increasing membership to try to wrest concessions on wage and working conditions from individual employers. The idea of nationally negotiated agreements had been unknown, and the unions themselves were regarded by 'respectable' society as being almost synonymous with criminal activity. These strikes cost the NUGGL dearly, strike benefits consuming most of its annual income, £11,000 out of £15,000, in 1892 alone. The gas workers, and most of the other unions, realised that basing their campaigns on the workshop floor alone was unlikely to achieve much without a parallel political effort.

By 1890 the 'new unionism' had spread rapidly across the industrial areas of the country. The gas workers were were in a bitterly fought campaign to achieve an 8 hour day. They had to organise strikes in several areas some of which were quite lengthy, especially in Leeds where 'blacklegs' had been hired to replace the strikers. It became an extremely bitter dispute, and the picketing gas workers threw missiles of all kinds at the 'blackleg' labour as they arrived for work.

This dispute became a test of strength, and later Will Thorne boasted that he would gladly have gone through it all again. When the strike ended in the unions favour, Friedrich Engels presented him with a copy of Marx's *Capital*, addressed to the 'victor of the Leeds battle.' This, and other successes, helped the gas workers to increase recruitment to their union in Lancashire and Yorkshire. It was also successful in recruiting workers from outside the gas industry, such as woollen textile workers in the West Riding.

A political party to represent the burgeoning labour movement was needed to strengthen and supplement their efforts. There had been a few manual workers elected to Parliament for industrial areas since 1874, often with the support of local Liberal Parties, and they took the Liberal whip, being known as 'Lib-Labs.' At the subsequent general elections their numbers increased, most of them ex-miners representing their own coalfield areas in Yorkshire, the North-East and South-Wales. These men impressed at Westminster with their dignity and working class voices, arguing in favour of industrial improvements. But they sat with the Liberals and were seen by the rest of the Labour movement as too timid and in thrall to the employers. They were also criticised for being a barrier to the creation of an independent labour party, and this argument was forcefully made at the Trades Union Congress by Keir Hardie, Ben Tillet, and Tom Mann among others. However, the TUC was not yet ready to endorse the creation of such a party, and at the 1888 conference voted against the setting up of separate political representation. But the movement for separate political representation gained ground both inside and outside the trade unions.

The move to form an independent labour party took place without the conversion of the trade unions. The delegates from the various strands that made up the labour movement attended a meeting in January 1893 at Bradford, with the aim of forming an Independent Labour Party. Although it later came to be seen as the moral conscience of the movement, the ILP was from the start a flexible group, and sought to embrace all the shades of left-wing opinion.

The over-riding aim of the ILP was to send working men to Parliament, and independent of the two main political parties. Many younger trade unionists joined, including Clynes and Pete Curran of the Gas Workers, who were both founder-members. Will Thorne was approached by Keir Hardie at the TUC congress in 1892 and asked if he would help promote the new party. Although he agreed with its objectives, he told Hardie he wished to remain a member of the Marxist Social Democratic Federation. In its infancy the ILP was able tolerate a broad membership including revolutionary socialists, with parallel membership of the SDF quite common. The ILP grew rapidly and had over three hundred branches by the end of 1893, including at Oldham in which Clynes was active.5

Through his trade union work, Clynes was sent to the International Socialist and Labour Congress held in Zurich in August 1893, as one of the sixty-five British delegates, one of the largest groups. He was impressed with the beauty of the Swiss lakes, and in Zurich met Bernard. Shaw. While swimming in the lake one day he 'saw a ruddy beard on the surface of the water,floating gently towards me...' They got into conversation on returning to shore, and Clynes found Shaw to be 'sincere and vital, still full of satirical .....truth and justice.'

But in the conference hall, he was unimpressed with the '....inflammatory verbal orgies of the representatives of certain Latin and Slavonic races...the vigour with which they disagreed among themselves would have been amusing had it not been somewhat dangerous' Shouting was a constant, and violence at times likely to erupt with a knife being flashed, and delegates 'fumbling as if for their revolvers.' Most of this uproar was caused by the presence of the anarchists, and a resolution was passed to expel them from the congress. Clynes felt that many of the disagreements arose from nationalist feelings due to the frustration with empires and long years of war. He took away a poor impression of European socialism, which he saw as negative and destructive in stirring up class war, while doing nothing constructive to improve the conditions of organised of labour.[6]

The industrial troubles came to a peak in Lancashire when the big mill owners proposed a 10% reduction in their worker's wages. They wanted to maintain profits that were being threatened by overseas competition. To many of the textile workers, already living on the bread-line, such a wage cut would mean starvation, and refused to accept the ultimatum. There was a universal 'lock-out' in all the mills at Oldham, and throughout Lancashire they were silent and the workers idle, left to stand around chatting on street corners.

The lock-out continued for five months until it was eventually settled by the compromise of a 3% wage cut, with all future changes in wages to be negotiated. This dispute did not involve Clynes's union, but he was still involved emotionally as many of his friends and union colleagues were affected. He was still learning his skills as a union negotiator, and the lesson of the mill lock-outs was to explore all opportunities for compromise and avoid ultimatums. The longer the duration of the lock-outs, the more suffering for the striker's families and the pressure to return to work under unfavourable conditions was enormous.

In 1895 there was a long strike at a Lancashire printing firm in Liverpool over wages and, although it did not involve his union, Clynes went to see the men with Bruce Glasier, a prominent ILP activist in the North West. The company had engaged a large number of 'blackleg' workers, mainly Scotsman who belonged to an anti-Labour organisation called the 'Free Labour Society'. They marched with a Union flag and drum and fife band into the works, but needed a large police escort to prevent violence from the angry strikers.

On arriving at the works gates, Clynes and Glasier found a crowd of people gathered. They passed through to take a look inside the works, had some lunch, and tried to speak with some strikers who unfortunately mistook them for blackleg agents. The pair were soon surrounded by an angry crowd. They asked if the pair were Scots and Glasier had to admit he was, and somebody threw a stone that just missed their heads. There were cries of 'Blacklegs' and 'Spies' and the situation was turning ugly. Clynes niftily climbed on to a low wall and told the crowd who they were and why they were there. They recognised the name of Glasier and his wife, Katherine St John Conway, who were both well known in the Labour cause in Liverpool. After Clynes had made a sympathetic and mollifying speech, the crowd became friendly, and invited them to return for a large public meeting the same night which was a great success.7

As a union negotiator, Clynes realised that the best way to secure settlements advantageous to his members was to see both sides of a dispute, so that all opportunity for compromise were explored. His method was to always be moderate and rational, while keeping the interest of his members uppermost in his mind. In his view there was no point in being implacably negative, opposing everything that owners wanted, so long as these did not detract from the core interests of his members.

Clynes considered dramatic displays of ' heroism' on behalf of the workers merely likely to exasperate the other side in negotiations, even if they might curry temporary favour with members. He regarded strikes as usually unprofitable on both sides, particularly as the lengthy ones plunged the families of strikers into penury and real suffering. The preference was always to seek the middle ground, and from there move as far in the desired direction as possible, as lasting settlements had to contain advantages for both sides so that neither could speak of total victory.[8]

Within a brief period he became a hardened negotiator, but just getting to the table was often dependent on the good will of the employers. They were were not compelled to meet a union representative, and many were bitterly opposed to the unions in the first place, often refusing to meet with representatives. In seeking contact with an employer in the early stages of a dispute, Clynes was therefore often met with rebuffs, and told no third party involvement in the dispute would be tolerated. But he was persistent and dogged in his determination to be recognised as the representative of his members, although never in a bellicose or strident manner. In meetings he never raised his voice, but gently put forward rational arguments in a reasonable tone, always seeking some middle ground as the basis for agreement. This talent for persuasion in face to face meetings was combined with an air of sweet reason and charm, sometimes amazing employers by quoting whole sections from the Bible or Shakespeare to illustrate a point. This kind of personal touch often helped to settle disputes and diffuse angry situations in which emotions were never far from the surface. The more settlements Clynes succeeded in obtaining, the more persuaded were both members and employers about the virtues of arbitration. This was especially true if a strike seemed intractable with both sides feeling the loss of revenue and income.

To make incremental gains in wages and working conditions was a cumulative process, one level leading to another. To aim for outright victory, or to claim it, was to Clynes counter-productive, and contained the seeds of future trouble. It left at least one side with feelings of resentment, which could fester and lead on to future problems. The aim should always be to establish trust and mutual respect, otherwise any agreement would be likely to prove unworkable from an industrial relations standpoint. At the same time, almost any agreement achieved by a new union was a huge step forward for its members, who had previously enjoyed almost no rights or security of employment, income or working conditions.

In 1896, Clynes became secretary for the whole Lancashire district, and his reputation as its organiser continued to grow. But in parallel to this work there was his proselytizing for the creation of a new Labour Party. This included trying to overcome the opposition to the party from many union members, who were still firm Liberal or Tory supporters. It was extremely difficult to gain election to the Oldham town council as a socialist, and so he decided to concentrate on the local Trades Council as a means of representing the working class.

These bodies were formed to coordinate trade union activity in a town or city, including Oldham. From the 1840s they tried to overcome trade union rivalries and present a common front of organised labour to problems, and to provide a debating forum for a wider range of issues than just employment. They eventually came to be important civic pressure groups on a range of economic, cultural, political and social issues as they affected the working class.10

In 1897 Clynes became President of the Oldham Trades Council which represented all the cotton operatives in the town, and gained further experience as a delegate to the Oldham Chamber of Commerce. Here, he sat with employers and small businessmen, learning more about their psychology and points of view. He often had to sit and listen to views about the workers that were hurtful to him, and with which he strongly disagreed, but after listening quietly and patiently, then triedto represent as best he could the views of those who had sent him there.

He was also still involved with the fledgling ILP and met many of it's leading figures when attending meetings and conferences . Among these, he was impressed by

Edward Carpenter, who was well known as a lecturer at
ILP and other socialist meetings, impressive with his
his flowing cloaks and wide brimmed hats, leading the
the processions while helping to finance several labour
groups. He came from wealthy family background, and
moved to the North in 1874 having been a curate and
become a Christian Socialist. In Sheffield he also became
increasingly radicalised and joined the SDF. Although his
utopian communitarianism had little in common with
trade union politics, his ethical socialism appealed more
strongly to Clynes.

Carpenter's hymn, 'England Arise!', became the
marching song of the Left until 'The Red Flag' was
adopted as the Labour anthem. Clynes always preferred
Carpenter's hymn with its dream of a pastoral England,
throwing off the chains of capitalist submission, and
Labour awakening to claim it's just reward, with its
closing verse:

> Forth then, ye heroes, patriots and lovers!
> Comrades of danger, poverty and scorn!
> Mighty in faith of Freedom, thy great Mother!
> Giants refreshed in Joy's new rising morn!
> Come and swell the song,
> Silent now so long;
> England is arisen, and the day is here!

In contrast, Clynes felt the 'The Red Flag' contained too
much bloody imagery with martial overtones that were
inappropriate for the English experience. Whereas, the
by Carpenter seemed to be rooted in England and in the
experiences of the working class.

peaceful socialist   idealism without resorting to class conflict.

Despite initial enthusiasm, the ILP did poorly in the general election of 1895 with all its candidates for parliament defeated, including Keir Hardie. And yet the the trade union movement was getting stronger, more class conscious, and convinced that a separate political party to represent labour was needed. Clynes and many others were pushing hard for this, and in 1899 at the the Trades Union Congress in Plymouth it was agreed that a Labour Representation Committee should created.

The resolution read that the aim of this body was:

'securing the better representation of Labour in the House of Commons' and instructed the 'Parliamentary Committee to invite all the Cooperative, Socialists, Trade Unions and other the working class organisations to cooperate on lines mutually agreed upon, in convening a special congress of representatives from such of the above mentioned organisations as may be willing to take part, to devise ways and means for securing the return of an increased number of Labour members to the next Parliament.' 11

There was a narrow vote in favour, and the support of the new unions was necessary. The gas workers stood together with the railwaymen, dockers, printers and boot and shoe operatives in carrying the vote against those unions such as the textile workers and miners who wanted to continue supporting the existing parties.

This led to a meeting at the Farringdon Memorial Hall in London on 27-28 February 1900 where the Labour Representation Committee was established. Clynes was present representing his union at this momentous event, where he met leading figures such as Philip Snowden and Ramsay MacDonald for the first time. However, it was by no means free from dispute, hardly surprising with so many shades of opinion present. There was particular conflict between the revolutionary SDF and those non-socialist trade unionists, such as George Barnes of the engineers union. The leaders of the ILP realised that the resources of the trade unions were needed, even if this meant compromising on their socialist aims. Clynes was in agreement with Hardie and MacDonald over this, and saw no contradiction between the pursuit of socialism and the representation of organised labour. He saw the two as wholly connected, for what was socialism if it did not lead to the improvement in working and living conditions of the working class.

The pursuit of socialism that was not grounded in this basic form of class solidarity was futile in Clynes's view, as was the attempt to reduce the new party to a group of organisations loosely attached to the interests of the working class. In the event, the new party was to have a loose federal structure and no leader, but a National Executive Committee consisting of seven trade union representatives, two from the ILP, two from the SDF, a Fabian Society representative and a secretary, an unpaid post that was filled by Ramsay MacDonald. The Gas Workers were represented on the NEC by Pete Curran, who was later joined by Clynes in 1904, wearing yet another hat, this time as the representative of the Trades Councils, being the secretary of one of the largest.

The new party was hardly in existence when a general election was called later in 1900, against the background of an imperial crisis in South Africa with British forces in retreat and the sieges of Mafeking and Ladysmith. The Tory government of Lord Salisbury sought to exploit feelings of patriotism created by this crisis, and win a vote of confidence from the people to pursue the war against the Boers more vigorously, even with the large number of casualties involved.

This 'Khaki' election was not an auspicious time for the new Labour party to contest its first elections, with divisions over the war and lack of resources to mount campaigns, even in the restricted number of seats being contested. Labour tried to concentrate on policies such as old age pensions, the nationalisation of the railways and mines, as well as social reform, but was drowned out by the jingoism surrounding the war issue. Several speakers at Labour meetings were stoned when they criticised the war, and mobbed by angry crowds, while some fifteen candidates decided it was wise to avoid mentioning the war at all.

All the Labour candidates standing were defeated, apart from Keir Hardie in Merthyr and Richard Bell in Derby. It was an inauspicious start, but at least Labour had its first presence in the House of Commons. No sooner was the election over, than the trade unions experienced the shock of the Taff Vale Judgement in 1901. This made the railwayman's union liable for the costs of a strike at the Taff Vale Railway Company in South Wales. This legal ruling seemed to put all trade union activity at risk, and was a considerable blow to a union's right to organise a strike, and the loss of immunity which they had long enjoyed. It made the need for the unions to have a separate parliamentary presence even clearer, and led to an increase in the number of trade unions and Trade Council affiliations to the LRC. Will Thorne urged all members of the Gas Workers Union to support LRC candidates at local and national elections, emphasising how important it was to have a 'strong working class political party in the House of Commons' to push for higher wages and less hours.9

The increased trade union affiliation generated more income, and allowed the NEC to offer a £200 a year salary to its MPs. Clynes gladly supported his colleague Thorne as he had long advocated closer links between the unions and the new party, especially as union resources made it possible to build up organisation, and at a local level to fighting elections more effectively. The winning of elections, even in favourable seats, would be difficult unless all local trade unions and Trades Councils were affiliated to the party, and funds made available to meet election costs.

The secretary of the LRC, Ramsay MacDonald, had meanwhile made an electoral agreement with Herbert Gladstone, the Liberal Chief Whip, by which the Liberals would stand down in seats in which Labour had the best chance of beating the incumbent Tory. Some Liberals took a benign view of Labour then, seeing it as the continuation of the old working class wing of the Liberal Party.

Although it was not supported by all of the members, the view of the Labour leadership was that if the Liberal

Party wanted to widen the arrangement, they were glad to agree while retaining their independence. The out- of this was Labour gains in by-elections at Clitheroe in 1902, and at Woolwich and Barnard Castle in 1903, that showed the effectiveness of Liberal and Labour co-op- eration. In other by-elections where Labour had stood against the Liberals, the results were mainly very poor. This made Ramsay MacDonald even more determined to pursue an electoral deal with the Liberals for the 1906 election.

Clyne's was kept busy in Oldham with his trade union work and getting more involved in local politics. The local LRC branch was not large at this stage, but its few members made up in enthusiasm what it lacked in numbers. In the 1901 local elections the party contested all eight wards in Oldham, with Clynes fighting the Waterhead ward. But he was defeated, as were all the other Labour candidates. Undaunted, the next year he contested a by election in the St. Mary's Ward but again he was defeated, although this time by a smaller margin margin. In 1905 he contested the Clarksfield Ward with the leader of the Conservative Group on the council as his main opponent and just failed to defeat him by a few votes. This patient persistence won Clyne's some respect in the town, even from his opponents, and all the while a stronger Labour presence in the town was being built up despite the problems faced by the party in small industrial places in Lancashire.

In towns like Oldham there was rivalry between the Irish Catholics and the Non-conformists, with many Conservative voters in the cotton industry, as well as Liberals in the engineering sector, with many voters supporting Irish Home Rule. Clyne's three attempts to become a Labour councillor in the town in the early 1900s showed that, despite having a majority of working class inhabitants, support for the Labour cause was far from solid, and other local factors could be more important than class interest. These defeats made him more convinced than ever that the Trades Councils would provide the best base for a working class political activism, especially when the trade unions and the Labour Party were difficult to organise.10

After failing to get elected to Oldham Council, Clyne's concentrated on his work as secretary of the Oldham Trades and Labour Council as an alternative forum for representing organised labour. He became its delegate to the Oldham Chamber of Commerce, which gave him more insight into industrial relations from the employer's viewpoint.

He would willingly listen patiently to the views of the local Tory and Liberal businessmen, many of them employers, who would often to sound off about problems with the workers. Then when all had spoken, Clyne's would put the case for labour with sweet reason to his captive audience of employees, never raising his voice and often employing irony to great effect. He usually kept the strength of his socialist views to himself in such company, and during union negotiations, and never let party rancour or prejudice show. He was a sk lled listener, waiting until everybody had spoken, heard all their arguments, while appearing in no hurry to reply.11

For Labour to make an electoral breakthrough in Lancashire, the role of the Liberals was crucially important, especially in the large number of two-member parliamentary constituencies. The problem was how to accept Liberal help without diluting the socialist faith, to be liberal enough to attract Liberal voters while remaining socialist enough to avoid appearing an appendage of Liberalism. But ever the pragmatist, Clyne's acknowledged that in Oldham 'our progress from a Socialist point of view has been slow, but we have reached the stage where the separate action of the ILP would do much harm'12 This was not the kind of message many in the ILP wanted to hear, seeing themselves as keepers of the socialist conscience. But it chimed well with MacDonalds more practical urgency of getting as many Labour MPs elected as quickly as was possible.

For some time Clynes had been contributing articles to the *Clarion* newspaper. This socialist weekly had been founded by Robert Blatchford, who was its first editor and a great campaigning journalist. His aim had been to set up a new socialist paper as a challenge to the largely Tory popular press of the time. He wanted the *Clarion* to address serious political issues while entertaining its mainly working class readers with entertainment, short stories, society gossip and the brilliant illustrations of Walter Citrine. For a time this was a highly successful mix and the paper built up a large circulation, and a fearless reputation. It provided a platform for many of the political figures of the day, and was widely read in the North-West, based with its editorial offices in the centre of Manchester.

Clynes's wrote articles about the need for industrial reform, and for strong Labour Party presence to bring about reform, doing what he could to spread the socialist message. It was a useful platform to spread his version of the socialist message, and a testament to Blatchford's editorial tolerance as he largely disagreed with Clynes's views. Blatchford was opposed to the creation of an all-embracing parliamentary socialist party, believing it would become too absorbed in inter-party manoeuvres and distracted from the goal of achieving a socialist society.

The *Clarion* had a clear mission, laid down by its founder, to convert the mass of the working population to equality and social justice no less, and was strongly influenced by a desire to dismantle industrial exploitation and by a return to pre-industrial self-sufficiency. These views, strongly influenced by William Morris, had echoes of a romanticised *Merrie England,* which was the title of a short book by Blatchford. When this was published in 1885, it became an unlikely worldwide best seller, spreading the socialist gospel with simple homespun examples that addressed an eponymous everyman called 'John Smith'.

In the *Clarion,* Blatchford allowed a wide range of views to appear, including those of the ILP, the Fabians, and revolutionary socialists. Apart from disagreeing with Clyne's he also largely opposed the views of the Fabians and other leading ILP members such as Keir Hardy, Ramsay MacDonald and Fred Jowett. He castigated the parliamentary arrangement with the Liberals, seeing it as proof that a parliamentary party would dilute the cause of socialism. But at least he did agree with Clynes on the fundamental need for a mass movement to convince the people about the virtues of socialism, and without this informative work of conversion the project would be unfinished and likely to fail in the long term.

By now Clyne's reputation had grown in the North-West, and he was approached by the St. Helens local party to stand as a Labour candidate in a soon-to-held parliamentary by-election. But it was not a promising seat, and he declined feeling that he was perhaps not ready to move towards a party political career. He gave way to James Sexton, who was defeated and gained only a few hundred votes. Clynes did what he could to assist the new party by addressing open air public gatherings, especially at Bogart Hole Clough, a large park-like open space in Manchester famous for its political meetings.

There was a solid Tory majority on Manchester City Corporation, and the councillors tried to get the Labour meetings banned on the grounds of trespass, warning that anyone who spoke there would be arrested and imprisoned. It had the reverse effect, for the next meeting attracted large crowds, and there were pledges to defy the corporation and to carry on holding meetings on what had been common land. The first speaker was arrested, and the second, but the next speaker was Emmeline Pankhurst, and the authorities were wary of arresting a woman, especially one as well known and connected as Mrs Pankhurst, and her huge meeting passed off without more incident. The next week Clynes made a vigorous protest about the imprisonment of his colleagues , but having allowed Mrs Pankhurst to remain free the authorities could hardly arrest him, so they looked the other way.13

At this time Will Thorne was also facing difficulties in South West Ham constituency in East London, largely because of his membership of the Social Democratic Federation. Although it had been given two seats on the Executive of the LRC, the SDF had withdrawn from the new organisation in 1901 because it did not regard the organisation as socialist enough. Thorne thought the union should create and support a Socialist Labour Party of its own, and in 1900 had run unsuccessfully as 'Socialist and Labour' candidate in West Ham. But in 1904 the LRC refused to allow him to do so again, and a tremendous row broke out in the local party which resulted in Thorne offering to stand down as the candidate, even though the SDF had a majority in the West Ham Labour Party.

At this point Clyne's stepped in a conciliator and tried to save the situation. He got a resolution passed at the Gas Workers Union Biennial Congress in 1904 which requested 'the various representatives promoting Will Thorne's candidature to South West Ham to assent to his running under the common title imposed on all candidates supported by the LRC.' As the majority of Thorne's local party members were also members of the Gas Workers, mainly from the large Beckton Gas Works, he thought they would accept a union directive. However, a special delegate meeting representing all groups in the South West Ham party met, and decided to run the election in their own way. The union tried to mediate again, and this time Clyne's was successful in persuading the local party to allow Thorne to remain as the local Labour parliamentary candidate.14

It was not long before Clynes was again approached to stand as a parliamentary candidate, this time in North-West Manchester. The invitation completely surprised him as he had made no effort to find a seat, or had much ambition to become an MP. But his local reputation, trade union activity, journalism, and public speaking had impressed, and Councillor Tom Fox, who led the delegation, was highly persuasive. And yet Clyne's again hesitated, pointing out that he had no money or organization. But Fox made it clear they wanted him personally, and the rest could look after itself. So he was adopted to fight the Tory-held seat, and was well aware it was going to be a difficult contest.15

4
At Least a Party

The 1906 General Election was a remarkable one for the fortunes of the Labour Party, as it was now officially called, and for Clynes personally. There were fifty-five Labour candidates standing, and he was one of the thirty-one who benefited from the electoral arrangement with the Liberals. In Manchester North-West it was a straight fight between the sitting Tory MP, Sir James Fergusson, and the Labour candidate. But it was always going to be an uphill struggle for a fledgling party with no organisation, money or even a rented committee room in the constituency. Fergusson had represented the seat for twenty-one years, had been a Cabinet minister, and was well entrenched with a good organisation.

The local Labour Party hastily managed to set up a primitive organisation of sorts, and had plenty of enthusiastic volunteers from the surrounding areas. They gladly gave up their free time, and even their wages, stuffing envelopes and canvassing door to door during the campaign. There was also help from the Liberals who had a previous presence in the seat, and who found common ground with Labour on the issues of free Trade and the repeal of the Taff Vale Judgement as well as welfare measures such as pensions.

But the seat was not solidly working class, and contained suburban lower-middle class voters. The Tory Party still had considerable advantages, and Clynes's main hope was to raise his profile high as he could with many mass public meetings, trying to get as much space as possible in the local press. The public meeting was the main form of political communication of the time, and the bigger the crowd the better for the candidates to reach as many as possible. One trick was to get a well-known or famous national figure to address the crowd in support, but Clynes had no famous speakers attending his meetings. Yet the 'David and Goliath' effect might have worked in his favour, and the support of many previously Liberal working people gave him a chance.

Clynes spoke at many meetings, in the open spaces, in hired rooms or in the streets of Ancoats. The meetings were generally packed and Clynes would speak, answer questions, and then move on to another meeting elsewhere with a cash collection at the end to help defray expenses. These were usually only half-pennies, but on one occasion a sovereign was discovered, a large sum perhaps equivalent to a whole weeks wages for a working man. An announcement was hurriedly made in case it had been a mistake, but no one claimed it. It was later discovered to have been contributed by a wealthy woman in the audience impressed with Clynes oratory, and who was converted to his cause and became a keen canvasser.[1]

The Manchester North-West constituency had always been a Tory seat, and the Liberals had suffered some crushing defeats there. The electors were unused to even having a candidate from a working class background, never mind from this new upstart Labour Party. As a consequence, Clynes suffered from this snobbery, as did many of the other Labour candidates. On one occasion, while out canvassing, he visited the house of a retired military officer who told him, 'I am a gentleman Mr Clynes and I have always been a gentleman, and a gentleman I intend to remain until my dying day. I consider it my duty, sir, to do my best to see that a gentleman is returned to Parliament for North-West Manchester.' He left Clynes in no doubt that he intended to vote for the Tory candidate. The notion of 'respectability' was still a potent force in late Victorian society, as was the importance of being a 'gentleman' in dress, manner and speech. Labour candidates, who were almost all working men, suffered from this social snobbery even if they were no longer working in manual occupations.[2]

A general election campaign was a major event and welcome distraction for the population of Manchester. It was a source of both interest and entertainment, with extensive local newspaper coverage. The candidates tried for every opportunity to get free publicity with public meetings and processions, many banners and a great deal of loud heckling. Manchester United Football Club even invited Clynes and Winston Churchill, who was standing in Oldham, having switched to the Liberals after many years as a Tory, to kick off for them in a big football match. In front of a huge crowd of some 70,000 spectators, Clynes kicked off the first half of the game, and Churchill the second half. After a match with some good football, United won the game which both candidates took to be a good omen.

At the count in Manchester North-East it seemed as if something surprising was happening as the votes piled up for Labour candidate, and Clynes could hardly believe it when he had won. A policeman on guard at the door to the counting room shook his hand, and asked to be the first to congratulate him. The result was a Labour majority of 2,432, a thumping win given the restricted electorate of the time and the disadvantages faced by Labour. There were wild scenes of delight and celebration among his supporters that continued well into the night, and the new MP shook so many hands they were aching by the time he departed for home.4

The 1906 national election result was an important breakthrough for the Labour Party with 29 MPs elected and 7,264,608 votes polled, trebling their vote of 1900. But it was even better for the Liberals who won with a landslide, and enjoyed a large majority in the House of Commons. The reality was that Labour would not have done as well without the electoral arrangement with the Liberals, and their support in many seats. This was particularly so in the North-West, where the Liberals were more willing to cooperate, and it resulted in thirteen Labour MPs elected for Lancashire and Cheshire seats. But the Party had shown it could win votes and seats from the Tories, espousing socialism and also Free Trade, popular among the Liberals and even among Tories in the mill towns. The Liberals sent a letter to some of the new Labour MPs trying to persuade them to return to the Liberal Party fold, and offering the possibility of a separate group of 'Lib-Lab' MPs within the Liberal Party.

Although the Liberals had a majority of eighty four,

the emergence of the Labour Party on the national scene was of considerable interest to the press. Only one of the twenty-nine Labour MP's, Will Thorne, was sponsored by the Gas Worker's Union but several other MPs who were officials of the union, including Clynes, were not. By the time Pete Curran was elected an MP in 1907 at a by-election in Jarrow, the Gas Worker's were the second largest trade union group in the House of Commons, and also the largest affiliated to the Labour Party for a time, until the miners joined in 1909.

His election to Parliament meant that Clynes had to be present when the new parliamentary session opened, but there was no question of maintaining two households. Therefore, he had to find a bed-sitting room in London as quickly as possible, which he did south of the Thames, and returned home to Mary and his two children at weekends. It would be difficult combining his trade union work with his parliamentary duties, which involved constant travelling between the North West and London. Rail travel at the time was considerably slower than to-day, and hours were spent on the London to Manchester line, often involving changes at Crewe. This entailed considerable expense, as did paying for his London accommodation in a somewhat seedy area of Lambeth, but in convenient distance of the House of Commons. But there were other expenses of living in London during parliamentary sessions, a tremendous burden at a time when MP were unpaid, and Clynes was totally dependent on his trade union salary. But it did not go far enough, and this soon became clear from a break-down of his expenses with daily costs including £1/4/0 bed and breakfast accommodation, 14 shillings meals, 3 shillings bus and train fares (in London), 6 shillings for postage costs, as well as clothes, rail fares between London and Manchester. This was in addition to supporting his wife and family in Oldham, so it was clear that he was going to be out of pocket each month, and have a struggle to make ends meet. However, these difficulties would have to be faced and overcome, and in any case there was no looking back now.5

When the twenty-nine new Labour MPs gathered for the first time in the House of Commons they engaged some administrative help, and elected Keir Hardie as their Chairman, effectively the new leader. They were allocated a room off one of the corridors, and elected a whip and some other officers who met daily while the House of Commons was in session. They also agreed to have a party meeting of all the MPs once a month to discuss plans of campaign, select speakers for debates and set up parliamentary committees. They sat as a group on the opposition benches, immediately to the Speaker's left, on the front two rows just below the gangway. Clynes immediately resented the ceremonial formalities that seemed designed to stifle the enthusiasm of the Labour members, to confuse them, and make them seem awkward. He decided to spend some time observing and absorbing the atmosphere of the place before making a maiden speech. To learn about the procedures and traditions of the Commons was a wise decision, but he must also have been rather intimidated in a House which contained so many famous figures of the time, such as Asquith, Lloyd George, and Balfour who was determined to try to re-build the Tory fortunes after a disastrous defeat. Clynes was impressed by some of the speeches he heard, if not their content, while others were decidedly poor and he knew he could do better. He was particularly impressed by Balfour, and learned from him the power of dignified self-restraint in the House that suited his personality, rather than emotional pontificating.6

Although Keir Hardie was regarded as the leader of the Labour group there was no official leader, and there was speculation about whether a formal leader was needed, who it should be, and what powers they would have. Soon after his election, Clynes was interviewed by the *Clarion* journalist Henry Beswick about the leadership issue. He was reported to have said that '.....we are no longer a few scattered individuals. We are at least a Party.....my own view is favourable to the appointment of a sessional chairman instead of a permanent leader.' He thought that the new Labour MPs would not be prepared to vote 'just as their leader tells 'em to', and that 'our party is made up of a number of leaders'.7

The trade union MPs, outside the ILP, had a distaste for Hardie or any other ILP contender. In any case Hardie did not find parliamentary leadership to his liking, and despite his virtues, was not in his element. He stood down in 1908, and was succeeded by Arthur Henderson. He stood down in February 1910, to be succeeded by George Barnes, with Clynes elected as the vice-chairman, a sign of the esteem in which he was already held by his colleagues and his good trade union links.

The kind of emotional rhetoric Hardie practised, and the scenes he occasionally made in the House, aroused little sympathy with most of the trade union MPs and the emotional rhetoric of others, such as Victor Grayson and Ben Tillet, even less so. Clynes thought this was often cheap oratory, and a distraction from their work, agreeing with Ramsay MacDonald that Grayson was 'making an utter fool of himself.'[8] As a new MP, there were many things to get used to, and one immediately affecting Clynes was the avalanche of mail he started receiving. Most of the letters were from constituents requesting help or some kind of favour, but others came from all kinds of correspondents giving their views on some issue or another. He tried to answer as many as possible, but with no secretarial help this was time-consuming.

There were other unforeseen problems, mainly to do with unavoidable expenses such as cab fares when kept late in the House because of a vote. The trains and buses would have stopped running, and he had to reach his bed and breakfast accommodation in the south London suburbs where he had moved to find even cheaper accommodation. But at least he could eat reasonably cheaply in the Member's Restaurant at the House of Commons with meat and two veg followed by a pudding or fruit, all at 1 shilling.[9]

The King's speech at the opening of Parliament was a great disappointment to the Labour group, with no mention of the promised old age pensions. While the workhouses for the destitute aged were costing over £14 million a year, it surely made sense to pay an old age pension of £5 a week as Labour proposed for all over 65 years of age. Clynes soon became bitter about the callousness shown by some MPs towards the poor, as well as their patronising and sometimes arrogant attitude to the new Labour MPs.

He began asking parliamentary question to ministers, and made his maiden speech in May 1906 in a debate on the eviction of workmen, a subject close to his heart and about which he knew a good deal. He outlined instances where striking workers families, mainly in the coal industry, had been evicted from their homes to try to force them back to work. There were many recent examples, such as at Hemsworth colliery where tents were erected on muddy ground to accommodate the evicted, with the rain pouring in and up to their ankles in mud, 'no grace or quarter was shown the suffering and starving people…...mothers had to sleep with children in their arms.' At the time 25% of miners lived in houses owned by the company, without any security of tenure. The speech was low key in his usual style with no rhetorical flourishes, outlining the facts and proposing reasonable suggestions, but with an underlying sense of moral purpose.10

The passage of the Trades Disputes Act was at least one promise the government enacted early, and was extremely important to the Labour Party as it effectively reversed the Taff Vale Judgement. Trade unions were now no longer liable for paying damages as a result of organizing strike action. It had risked bankrupting the unions, and nearly curtailed their freedom in disputes. Despite this there was still initial disillusion with the government, and impatience with them for not making their promised social reforms immediately. This applied also to women's suffrage, which Clyne's and colleagues had long supported. He gave help to the Pankhurst's in Manchester, speaking at meetings in support of their Women's Social and Political Union.

When the suffragists discovered that the Liberal win did not lead to their demands being met, they took to more violent methods of protest, with many arrests and convictions following for disorderly conduct. Clynes made several interventions on the subject in the Commons, for example protesting to the Home Secretary about the treatment of a suffragette protester in Manchester. She was still in prison after being arrested at a peaceful protest in London, while others who were present were allowed to go free. And he also spoke out against the injustice of several long prison sentences imposed, as suffragettes started using more militant methods of protest and demonstration such as smashing shop windows and chaining themselves to public buildings.[11]

Neither Clynes nor Thorne made much distinction between their trade union and parliamentary work, seeing the latter an extension of their tasks promoting the cause of the unskilled and semi-skilled manual men.

They took every opportunity to speak on all issues they thought affected their members, or might do so in the future, such as unemployment. This was one of the few subjects about which Clynes allowed himself to become emotional. To both men, the Labour Party was part of the wider labour movement, which included the trade unions and other representative bodies. At the Labour Party conference in 1909, Clynes elaborated his views on this by making clear he thought the PLP's main function was to push for improvements for organised labour:

> The socialist is left entirely free to pursue his business in the politics of the country, and is able to do his work to greater advantage by its contact with the organised workers who are in their trade unions in no way hampered but helped by the alliance in their industrial duties which called them into being. The trade unionist asks for a share of the wealth he creates, and the socialist encourages him to claim the full product of his labour and calls upon all who are able to do so to give their share of service for their share of wealth.12

The initial disillusion with the Liberal government abated by 1908, as the Liberals recovered their reforming agenda. They introduced old age pensions for which Labour pressured hard and which, together with the Trades Disputes Act, brought the trade union Labour MPs and the Liberals closer together. This may also have reflected the fact that the many of their members, and some officials still voted Liberal or Conservative, and their political position was still not secure.

This was revealed when a Liberal-voting minor official of the railway men's union, W.V. Osborne, had challenged his union's right to use their member's funds

1. A view of Oldham in the late nineteenth century

2. Spinners and a Piecer in an Oldham cotton mill c. 1880

3. David Lloyd George

4. Will Thorne

5. ILP Poster 1895

6. Clynes defends the worker's beer

for political purposes. The courts upheld his complaint which much reduced the trade unions funding of the Labour Party until political levies were made legal in 1913.

This was another potential blow to the Labour Party, but Clyne's opposition to the Osborne Judgement was also based on the argument that the Labour Party now reflected, and reinforced, the growing importance of organised labour in society. The workers had the right to have their own representation in the House of Commons, whatever prejudices this might arouse, and that the trade unions had a right to finance their political voice. He believed that 'the political opinions of workmen should be respected and these opinions will be fairly dealt with by the workmen's mates, if only scared politicians will allow the members of trades unions and the various branches of the Labour Party to settle their own business.13

In March 1908 Clynes introduced into the House of Commons a motion for an 8 hour working day, declaring that 'the time has arrived when the interests of the worker's generally, and in the view of the present large number of unemployed, the working day in all trades and industries should be limited by law to a maximum of 8 hours.'14 He went on to point out that salaried and skilled workers had more or less already achieved an 8 hour day, and that he was arguing in favour of equity and fairness. He gave examples from the three industries of coal mining, textiles and railway, and showed how the employers' arguments against an 8 hour day were generally absurd and invalid, ignoring the dangers and difficulties of the workers in these industries and its reflection in their pay rates. He argued that 'industrial workers ought not to be worked so hard, paid such meagre wages, or treated so badly as they are today.'15

The prospect of an eight hour day was viewed with alarm by those MP's who were themselves employers, related to employers or who were supported by the employers. A petition had recently been submitted by members of the Gas Workers Union, who worked for a large employer in Lancashire who was also a Tory MP, for an increase in wages and a reduction in the working day. Someone had attached Clyne's name to this document without his knowledge and one day the MP, a martinet with military rank, stopped him in a Commons corridor and upbraided him as if in a court martial. Clynes tried to explain he had had nothing to do with the petition, but was told to be silent.

The affronted MP threatened to go to the editor of a Manchester paper and accuse Clynes of sowing discontent between employers and management. Clynes told him he would be glad to meet him in his constituency to discuss the issue at any time, and the Tory stomped away muttering angrily. He then wrote a letter to the local paper complaining about the employer's discourtesy, and asking for a meeting on any public platform. There was silence and his union did eventually obtain improved wages and conditions in that dispute.16

The Liberal government's reforms may have placated

the trade union members, but the Left wing in the Labour group were far from impressed, and the emotional oratory of Victor Grayson and Ben Tillet continued. Their uncompromisingly socialist agenda involved an intransigence of which Clynes disapproved, and which he still saw as self-indulgence and self-defeating. He even went so far as to suggest that the Labour Party did not have to be an exclusively socialist party, but should be open to all people of goodwill who loosely shared Labour's aims.

Never happy under Keir Hardie's leadership, Clynes got on better with Arthur Henderson with whom he generally agreed. At the 1908 Labour Party conference Clynes spoke against a motion, proposed by Ben Tillett, that sought the adoption of a policy to obtain for the workers 'the full results of their labour by the overthrow of the present system of capitalism and the institution of a system of public ownership and control of all the means of life.' In the speech he told delegates that, although he believed in the public ownership of distribution, production and exchange, he did not believe they should sharpen the weapons of the enemy by aiming for too much too soon. The people had to be converted to the socialist cause first, fighting elections on an uncompromising socialist agenda was futile otherwise. Labour should use its 'energies to existing political opposition' so to 'bring the best fruit and most helpful matter to the working class of the land'[17]

He believed the people could best be converted to socialism by seeing the benefits of social and economic reform working in practice to their benefit, that people had to see that their self-interest lay in more equality and cooperative enterprise. In this way they could come to realise that the Labour Party was their best chance of seeing a society reformed through socialism. In the meantime, the trade unions should continue with their pressure for improved wages and working conditions, by strike action if necessary, and contribute to the same ends as the Labour Party. To an extent this is what happened between 1906 and 1914, as increasing strikes and industrial actions were accompanied by a rise in support for the Labour Party. However, the project remained uncompleted, as there was no systematic or well organised effort of education and information at the grassroots level, and large sections of the working class remained unconvinced and were never converted to the socialist cause.

The collaboration between Labour and the Liberal government continued to produce social reforms, which benefited working class voters who supported both parties. In 1907 medical inspection in schools was introduced, and the provision of school meals by local authorities was encouraged. These were largely due to agitation by the Labour Party in Bradford, where the party was strongly entrenched under the leadership of Arthur Henderson, and by Labour MPs. The Coal Mines Act finally introduced the eight-hour day for miners, largely due to the pressure of the Miner's Union supported by Labour MPs, and Labour Exchanges set up in 1909. Lloyd George proposed levying on the unearned income of the wealthy and on their motor cars, as well as preparing the ground for a land tax by a national valuation of land holdings. These radical measures were partly intended to attract working class support, as well as to placate the Labour Party and to ensure its support. It raised the issue of whether the Labour Party should continue with a policy of close co-operation to extract such reforms or to break up with the Liberals entirely and pursue its own purer socialist agenda.

At the 1909 Labour Party conference in Plymouth, Clynes was the chairman, and there were efforts made by Victor Grayson and others on the left to try to disrupt Lib/Lab cooperation, and commit the party to a pure socialist agenda. But they were in a minority, and the majority of the trade unionists continue to oppose them. In any case by 1910 a strong case could be made for the Labour strategy having been a success with a whole battery of social reforms. The fifteen Lib-Lab MPs had come over to Labour Party, there had been several by-election victories, and the party membership had increased from 500,000 to 1.5 million in ten years.

When the Lloyd George's controversial Budget was rejected by the House of Lords, Prime Minister Asquith decided to call an election in January 1910 after a resolution in the House of Commons declared the action 'a breach of the constitution'. This presaged a major constitutional crisis, and the election was called essentially so that the government could obtain a clear mandate from the people to pass the budget. But public opinion was deeply divided over the wisdom of the Liberal course, and the Tories under Arthur Balfour won the largest number of votes although the Liberals gained the largest number of seats. Labour continued its successful progress, and won forty seats, an increase of eleven over 1906 with an increased share of the vote. Clynes was re-elected in Manchester North East, but with a reduced majority of 1,478 in another straight fight with the Tories. It was clear that in an unpromising seat for Labour there were not enough working people willing yet to vote socialist, and some Liberal supporters unhappy with either the policies or tactics of the parliamentary leadership switched to the Tories.

The election did nothing to resolve the situation, and Asquith had to form a government with the support of Labour and the Irish Nationalists led by John Redmond. The situation was untenable, and another election was held in December 1910. During the hiatus between the two polls, Clynes accepted an invitation to visit the United States and Canada as a 'fraternal delegate' to the American Federation of Labour Convention. It involved a long week sea crossing, and it seems strange he should have taken a month away from British politics at such a frenetic time. But it was an opportunity he did not want to miss to see labour relations in North America at first hand, and cement good relations with the burgeoning American trade union movement. It would also mean a well-deserved holiday for Mary who had been stuck in Manchester for four years.

When they finally landed in Canada they spent a few days learning about the trade union scene there, and Clynes and his wife also found themselves the guests at a large gathering of Lancashire folk who had settled in Canada. On entering the hall, the whole audience rose and sang 'For She's a Lassie from Lancashire,' which, together with the warm welcome, deeply affected them both.[18]

They crossed the border to attend the AFL Convention, held that year in St Louis Missouri. While socialists were not prevented from joining, the AFL refused to support the setting up of a separate political party to represent labour, though it had grown closer to the Democrats since 1908. Clynes was amazed at the scenes in the convention hall when Samuel Gompers was re-elected President of the AFL, with the noise of cheering delegates and the applause. Gompers was a charismatic personality with a commanding presence and great vitality, his speech lasting over four hours while he smoked several cigars pacing up and down the platform. Clynes was invited to address the audience, and he could only manage an hour and a half, after which there was a noisy clamour for him to continue. He told the audience about the state of British labour relations and the successful pressure for old age pensions and workers compensation, and the role of trade unions in British politics. It was well received, but the contrast with a TUC conference could not have been more marked, having more of a carnival atmosphere in which delegates were determined to enjoy themselves.[19]

After this the Clynes travelled to several other places in America and visited recent immigrants in their homes, as well as schools, dockyards and factories. They were most impressed with Washington DC, and especially the beauty of the buildings, and visited the Senate and Congress. Yet despite the classical beauties of the White House and the statues of liberty, Clynes was constantly reminded that the workers still had no vote, graft and corruption was everywhere and even though wages were high, job security was low in an almost entirely free market economy. Although they enjoyed the beauty of the country and the hospitality of the people, the main lesson Clynes took away from this visit was the danger of allowing unfettered free markets to become the norm, and the importance of having a strong state able and willing to intervene to regulate the economy through policy and through a strong state-run sector of basic industry.20

The visit had to be fairly brief for at home a second election had been called by Asquith in December 1910. After the relaxation of the cruise home, Clynes was thrown back into the maelstrom of another election campaign. Henderson had resigned in February to be replaced by George Barnes of the engineering union, who was more acceptable to the majority of trade union MPs. Clyne's seat was increasingly marginal with no certainty he could hold it, and he needed to campaign vigorously. The expense of political campaigning was increasing, and the traditional large public meetings had more than ever to be supplemented with personal canvassing of every household in the constituency, as well as also distributing leaflets to every one of them. It was a briefer campaign this time, and had much more urgency with the need to break the political deadlock. It was just bitterly fought, however, and in some of the Manchester seats local employers even sat outside the polling booths to exert silent pressure on their workers. Clynes just managed to scrape home with a wafer-thin majority of only 205, less than 3% of those who voted. Over the rest of the country Labour increased its representation slightly, but its share of the poll was down from 31.6% to 29%.

The Liberals under Asquith again hung on to power, but the deadlock was not broken and they were again dependent on the support of the Irish Nationalists. Labour had failed to make further electoral progress, and there was soon criticism from the ILP about the strategy of supporting the Liberals. They argued for more socialist policies and a new strategy to achieve them. On the other hand, the electoral deal with the Liberals to once again restrict the number of three-cornered contests had succeeded in limiting the number of Conservatives elected, possibly preventing them from forming a government. Clynes with most of the other trade union MPs, and others like MacDonald, were still satisfied that the alliance had delivered a good deal with considerable social reform and with the scope for more tocome.21

After the Parliament Act of 1911 was passed depriving the Lords of its financial powers, the Liberal government decided to press forward with further reform, supported by Labour. It proposed urgently needed changes to the structure and organization of the army, increasing its size, and passed the long awaited National Insurance Act Act. Labour also welcomed the introduction of payment of MPs in 1911, with an annual salary of £400, and of great value to the party. Even with his salary as a trade union official, Clynes found living in London a costly struggle, but it would now be easier to afford the rent on separate accommodation in the capital.

MacDonald was the logical choice for the leadership and, although initially reluctant, he had qualities the other contenders lacked. He was a tall, handsome and impressive figure with a wonderful voice, effective in speeches both in the more intimate atmosphere of the House of Commons and in large halls or open-air public meetings. He had written many books and pamphlets and was had intellectual influence in the party. He was also capable of making strong socialist appeals when necessary and was generally associated with left, but never succumbed to making emotional protests in the House like Grayson. Despite his failings, which became so evident later, Clynes supported him as he seemed to be the best person for the job and had negotiated the agreement with the Liberals, showing considerable skill.

Labour continued to support the Liberal government, especially as it was promoting policies that Labour had itself pioneered, such as social insurance and MP's pay. Although it was not a formal coalition, it appeared to some on the left, particularly in the ILP, as if the Labour MP's group was being treated like junior members of an alliance in which the Liberals made all the running. This remained a problem in the years leading up to the First World War, as discontent became more evident among the rank and file membership. They wanted Labour to be more distinctive and to offer the electorate a clearer socialist choice. But Clynes supported MacDonald in believing that Labour had a duty to extract every last ounce of advantage from a vulnerable Liberal government, even though the long term goal should be to replace it as a party of government. He also agreed with MacDonald that, as the time for this had not yet arrived, a pragmatic strategy was best so long as the parliamentary situation made it possible, and the working class derived some benefit.

At the same time, Labour was still free to advocate policies such votes for women which the Liberals still opposed, and voice its independence in foreign and defence policy. But Clynes felt that so long as circumstances gave a good chance for the Conservatives to form a government, even on a minority of the votes, then it was safer to remain in some kind of arrangement with the Liberals. Many on the Labour side agreed with the Liberals that the best way of preventing this from happening was through electoral reform, and the introduction of some kind of proportional representation. This was adopted by the TUC, several trade unions, and the ILP at its 1913 conference, where Philp Snowden assured the delegates it would enable Labour to gain a hundred extra seats. But the bulk of the movement remained unconvinced. MacDonald was opposed, not least because he foresaw dozens of militant socialist candidates being elected without the need to placate local Liberal Parties in two-member seats. And yet despite his adherence to inter-party cooperation, and pessimism about replacing the Liberals as the main party of opposition to the Tories, he still supported electoral reform as it might hasten this prospect.

As well as his parliamentary work, Clynes was kept busy on trade union work. He was often called upon to mediate in industrial disputes where his skills as a mediator were thought to be exceptional. These pre-war years saw considerable industrial unrest and the militant union wing, led by Tom Mann and A.J. Cook, the minersleader, were attempting to get the Labour Party to break its links with the Liberal government. These union leaders despised the Labour Party for its timidity, and regarded its leaders as not being socialists at all. They were influenced by syndicalist ideas from abroad, and hoped to form a single union for each main industry.

They sought to use the weapon of a general strike to end capitalism, and secure the revolutionary overthrow of the old order. They had considerable influence for a time, and there were widespread strikes by the miners, railwaymen and other key workers. The employers responded with lock-outs of their workers with 120,000 being locked out in the cotton industry in 1910 alone.

Clynes was among those whom the militant union leaders held in low regard, and he made no secret of his opposition to their views and tactics. He had recently been appointed President of the Gas Workers Union, and used all his influence to keep militant ideas at bay, but even local branches of his union, the local leadership was growing increasingly militant and more willing to strikefor improved wage and conditions. Gas workers wereoften in dispute with the private gas firms as well as localauthorities, and a particularly serious dispute arose atLeeds in 1913 when 4,000 of the local Corporation workers had gone on strike. The NUGGL was involved with other unions and when local mediation failed to secure a settlement, Clynes was called on to help settle an escalating dispute. The local services were affected with only a skeleton tram service, limited gas supplies, no waste collection or street lighting.

The workers had a good case, and were united in their cause, but the Tory and Liberal councillors on the Corporation combined to break the strike. They were determined to concede nothing to the men, and just wait for a drift back to work. This eventually started to happen, but many gas workers stayed firmly united. Clynes was locked into four days of negotiations, but failed to get those still on strike reinstated as part of the final settlement. He was heavily criticised for making too many concessions to the employers and for allowing those still on strike to be cut adrift.

It seemed to many in the union movement that Clynes was now more of a neutral conciliator instead of a trade union champion. Although this view was not shared by the NUGGL members, the employers did see him as someone with whom they could work. Because of this reputation he was also co-opted in September 1913 by the Board of Trade to sit on a commission of enquiry into the Dublin Corporation tram workers strike.

The Irish TGWU failed to get the British TUC to call out workers in sympathy, and eventually the Irish workers were forced back without achieving their aims. This was a bitter strike and lockout, a highly politicised dispute in which it was difficult to disentangle genuine industrial grievances from political motives, and made worse by the recalcitrance of the employers.22 To Clynes the dispute was an object lesson of the dangers for organised labour of getting involved in a dispute without having areas in which they were willing to compromise. By going for broke, calling all-out strikes and waiting for the workers to be starved back to work was futile, and needed to be avoided. The employers and workers were involved in a partnership, each interdependent, and the recognition of this fact should be the basis of all good industrial relations.

The goal of union amalgamation emerged in these years of labour unrest, and Tom Mann set up 'Amalgamation Committees' to campaign for single industrial unions. There was considerable opposition to this from the powerful craft unions, and even from some general unions. By 1912 Thorne was advocating the merger of all the general unions into a single General Labourers Union, but the problems were considerable as Clynes explained:

> We have industrial conditions which place different grades of men in superior and subordinate relationship to each other.....it is futile to talk of forcing all these men into one organisation as though the fact of tradesman and labourers did not exist at all.....Labourer's unions cannot, with advantage,

be merged at present in the other unions; they can amalgamate their own forces and seek friendly alliance with other forces.23

But the advantages of size were still considerable, and the goal of merger continued to be pursued by the larger unions. The NUGGL put forward detailed proposals for amalgamation at a special conference of the Union's National Council which was chaired by Clynes. The other unions were less enthusiastic, and still failed to agree. In July 1914, a joint meeting took place at which thirty-one unions were represented, and they approved a common plan of amalgamation. The outbreak of war meant that these plans had to be deferred and were never properly taken up again.24

Finally another great obstacle to trade union rights influence was removed when the Osborne Judgement was reversed by the Trade Union Amendment Act in 1913, which Labour had been urging on the government for some time. It was now possible for the trade unions to use their funds for political purposes, if a majority of members agreed by a secret ballot. Although any member was allowed to 'contract out' of paying into the political fund the new law was a relief for the unions and the Labour Party which was under considerable financial pressure. While to Clynes it seemed to be yet another example of successful Labour pressure and co-operation with the Liberal government producing results to the benefit of the Labour movement, the militant unionists saw it as an example of the government dictating union 'rights.'

5
War Years

There had been a threat of war with Germany for some time, and when it was finally declared in August 1914 the Labour Party was as unprepared as the other political parties. Clynes was opposed to war until the very last minute, and moved towards supporting it with the majority of the party which was generally patriotic, and prepared to support a war to defend what it saw as the national interest.

But a vociferous minority, mainly in the ILP, remained strongly opposed to war. They included such important figures as MacDonald and KeirHardie, with their moral objections to war based on deeply held pacifist views. The majority of the trade union's accepted the argument of the government that Britain's imperial and strategic interests would be at risk if Germany was permitted to occupyFrance. To some extent they also reflected an upsurge in patriotic and nationalist feelings of the time, but there was also, contrary to popular myth, considerable foreboding among people about the war as they feared it would not not end quickly. Clynes shared these fears, but many Labour MPs were swept along by a patriotic 'war fever,' with Will Crooks even rising in the packed House of Commons to spontaneously start singing the National Anthem at the announcement of hostilities.

The Labour Party Executive held a meeting on the 4th August 1914, at which they discussed the policy position.

After criticizing the government handling of the situation they decided to support the war effort. Clynes thought that having reached the stage 'where our protests could not keep 'England' out of a war which was already in existence, we could serve her better by an unswerving, if protesting, loyalty.' MacDonald dissented from this view, resigned as chairman, and Arthur Henderson took over again. A split was avoided and the anti-war group members on the NEC remained in post but in any case the majority of Labour voters were by this time fully supportive of the war. This was true in Lancashire where Clynes was soon made aware of working class patriotic feelings. They which began to run high, and thousands of young men, many from the textile industry, flocked to volunteer for army service. Clynes approved, and even encouraged, this patriotic feeling, believing it showed a deep love of country that superseded any party political commitment.1

The response to Lord Kitchener's call for volunteers led to the formation of the so-called 'Pals Battalions' based on mill towns such as Accrington, Chorley, Burnley and Manchester, all attached to the East Lancs regiment. They were sponsored by the local Mayors and councils but were largely spontaneous, and most of the young men who volunteered were later killed on the battle fields of Flanders. The scale of this loss of life could hardly have been envisaged at the time, and at the Battle of the Somme in July 1916 most of the Accrington lads were wiped out on the first day. The realities of modern warfare, not fully realised in 1914, were to be blindingly clear by 1916.

The wave of working class patriotism in 1914, with which he sympathised and shared, was one reason why Clynes strongly supported the war. Most of the voters in Manchester, Oldham and other towns in the North West supported it, as Clynes was not slow to remind the party. He argued that his view 'was consistent with the actions of a socialist, when the choice is no longer between peace and war, but between peace and submission to the warmaker.'2 But he still had some form of struggle with his conscience, as he came to realise that war meant an effective death warrant for many, even though at this stage he did not foresee the scale of the destruction and death that was to emerge as the war proceeded. But the early rapid advance of the German army, as he saw it, meant that the choice now was between resistance or surrender.

The appeals to the international solidarity of all the working class against the war mongering ruling classes had little appeal for Clynes, as his socialism was mainly based on what he saw as the interests of the British working class and it was their feelings that concerned him the most. Just as Blatchford and the *Clarion* saw the war as necessary to defend the values of native socialism rooted in the soil of England, so Clynes also saw no contradiction between socialism and patriotism. And as soon as the conflict began so his patriotism finally took precedence over any anti-war feelings he may have had.

The early military setbacks on the Western Front did nothing to alter this view, but emphasised that the war needed to be pursued even more forcefully. There were

Labour MPs who contributed to the recruiting drive by travelling all over the country speaking at meetings, encouraging young men to join up, and these included Clynes, Will Thorne, Will Crooks among others. At one such meeting in Manchester, Clynes own son Jack, by now an army lieutenant, presented an early VC to a local man called Private Stringer. But as it became clear that recruiting volunteers was not going to be sufficient, given the huge number of early fatalities, conscription seemed a certainty. Will Thorne supported it despite a son serving on the Western Front, who was later killed at Ypres. Thorne even joined the West Ham Volunteer Force himself, and held the rank of Lieutenant-Colonel of which he was proud, and gave further ammunition to his anti-war critics.

Despite this, when a Conscription Bill was introduced into the House of Commons in January 1916 the Labour Party opposed and fought it all the way. To Clynes there was an important distinction between volunteering for military service, and being forced to fight. To working class families, conscription would mean the loss of the main bread-winner, perhaps permanently, and a plunge in living standards. There would also be the problem of claiming the right to exemption through conscientious objection, and the denial of this right in many cases. For some socialists, like Crooks and Blatchford, the war should have had a unifying effect on the whole of the community faced with foreign aggression, and had an inherent social value. In addition, the sacrifices involved in answering the call to fight for 'King and Country' had be well very rewarded at the peace. The expectation was that when the war ended the loss of life, and all the sacrifices it had entailed for the mass of the working class would be recognised with large-scale social and economic reform.3

For some time Clynes had been taking on increasing responsibility for the family of his sister, who had been married to Harry Parker, a mill-hand from Oldham. He had died when the children were young, and she was on the verge of falling into poverty. Clynes came to the the rescue by helping financially and in other ways by taking a special interest in his nephew, Herbert, to whom he assumed an almost quasi-parental role into adulthood. Like Clynes's own son Jack, he joined up and served on the Western Front, experienced all the horrors of trench warfare, and was wounded. He was home to convalesce while Clynes and Mary helped him to adjust to civilian life. Herbert was an able young man, and Clynes helped finance his studies in at Christ's College Cambridge when he was invalided out of the army in 1918. Despite his abilities, the war had may have affected him psychologically, as it did so many others, for after only a year of study he dropped out.4

During the first two years of the war the Labour Party was supportive but critical of the government, and as the casualties mounted patriotism began to have its limits. Although strong criticism continued from MacDonald, Fred Jowett and other ILP members, the bulk of the parliamentary Labour Party continued to be supportive. Clynes was offered a place on the Munitions Workers Health Committee, dealing with issues such as exposure of munitions workers to picric acid. Increasing numbers of these workers were women, many experiencing life in factories for the first time. Clynes's experience with industrial safety matters was regarded as an asset, and he established good relations with Lloyd George who was Minister of Munitions at the time. He tried to do what he could to mitigate the health dangers of arms workers, but it became more difficult as pressure for increased production became relentless as the conflict went on.

In 1915 Clynes led a delegation from several large Midlands arms factories to view the battlegrounds at first hand. They travelled for three weeks across the devastated battlefields of France and Belgium, and saw the appalling effects of modern warfare. They passed through Ypres, once a pleasant ancient town, but now a mass of ruins full of collapsed buildings and rubble. They watched a British battery at work bombarding the German lines, and spoke with the artillerymen. The gunners were angry at the stories they had heard from home about war profiteering, and told the delegation about the injustices caused by bombs exploding prematurely due to cheap materials.

They spoke to an officer who told them the quality of the shells they recently received had improved, but complained about the shortages. This led to even more casualties because in the attack following a barrage the infantry had to cope with German barbed wire, which the artillery had been unable to damage because of lack of shells. The advancing soldiers were caught in the wire, or delayed in breaking through and were easy

targets for the German barrages. The delegation walked
through the trenches and saw the awful conditions. The
screeching whining of the shells overhead was extremely
frightening until they got used to it, and there were
several explosions nearby and falling shells. When they
were due to leave for home, Clynes noted the 'fatalistic
acquiescence' of the soldiers, their sadness at not being
able to leave with them for the peace of England and the
feeling they were just waiting to die or get wounded.[5]

The criticism of the majority of Labour MPs who
supported the war continued on the left of the party,
and Will Thorne and Clynes were bitterly attacked
in the *Labour Leader* by Philip Snowden. But their
trade union continued to support them over the war,
and at its 1916 Biennial Congress gave Thorne a standing ovation. But the *Labour Leader* also attacked the
NUGGL for neglecting to support a Lancashire District
organiser, Charles Dukes, who had been conscripted
despite being a conscientious objector and been court
martialed when he resisted for breaching the army's
discipline. But Clynes pointed out to the NUGGL
General Council that Dukes had written to Thorne to
thank them for their efforts in trying to gain exemption
for him.[6]

Despite sometimes bitter disagreements Clynes was
still, surprisingly perhaps, a member of the ILP but the
relations were becoming even more strained and he did
not attend the annual conference in Norwich in 1915.
Instead he wrote a letter to the chairman of the party
in which argued that support for the war was the right
one decision:

'....when the choice was no longer one between peace and war,
but war or submission to the war-maker. Socialists always called
for strong action by the government when the weak and
innocent in other lands were oppressed. The ILP now says
rightly that Belgium must be freed. How can we say so, and
leave that enormous task to other peoples?'[7]

He got no reply but continued as a member of the ILP as there was no effort to expel him. Although Clynes and Thorne with many other union leaders supported the war in principle, they had some self-interested motives in doing so. They realised that it put them in a stronger position to improve the conditions of their members, and to exert more influence politically both during and after the war. Neither did they feel restrained by the national emergency in expressing their convictions, or to point out the class conflicts that arose on the Home Front.

In December 1914 Will Throne was attacking the bankers, railway directors and dividend-receiving classes, 'those with huge fortunes who are fleecing the poorest people.' He and Clynes then went on the attack with the favourite theme of profiteering they alleged was rife among ship owners, colliery owners, wholesale wheat and meat merchants who were 'extracting millions out of the pockets of the poor by jumping the prices of food and fuel.'

Throughout 1915 and 1916 they asked many parliamentary questions about prices and profiteering, making contrasts between the contribution to the war effort of the working classes compared to the upper classes on the Home Front. They also pointed out the physical exhaustion of the workers in war production.

When the rich spoke of sacrifices, 'let us remind them of what the workers, their wives and children are silently doing for the country in this terrible struggle.'[8]

The mounting casualties on the Somme, the stalemate in the West, Gallipoli, and the Battle of Jutland, all made it clear that the war was not going to end quickly. Once this was apparent to both Asquith and Lloyd George, they realised it would be an advantage to include Labour more formally in the war effort. In May 1915 Asquith invited the Labour Party to join the coalition government. Clynes argued that Asquith was not making enough of an offer for Labour to justify participation, but it was a minority view. He and Will Thorne saw as a condition of any arrangement that the arms industry at least should be taken wholly into public ownership, not merely have its profits controlled by the Munitions Act that was passed a few months later. Despite a good deal of opposition to joining the government within the Labour Party, the National Executive voted in favour. Arthur Henderson joined the Cabinet as President of the Board of Trade, with a few other Labour MPs taking up junior posts.

Despite this new political unity, strikes continued in industry, and the general unions which included the Gas Gas Workers and General Labourers, as it now was, which had increased its recruitment of unskilled workers workers. The Munitions Act introduced the compulsory arbitration of disoutes, so trade unions could now force employers to negotiate with them. The NUGGL became the champion of the lower paid in the munition industry and secured the same pay rates or those employed in the jobs previously done by skilled labour.

In 1917 Clynes and Thorne campaigned hard for a reversal of the 'trade card' system by which only skilled workers could be exempted from military service. They felt this was unfair to the unskilled, particularly after the introduction of conscription, and throughout 1917 the pair continued their campaign with speeches and many parliamentary questions. They sent letters to the War Office and to the Ministry of Munitions and Directorate of National Service, as well as directly to Henderson in the Cabinet. They wanted all workers to enjoy equity of treatment, irrespective of their union, whether skilled or unskilled. In May 1917 they were finally successful and the trade card system was abolished, to be replaced by a system of 'reserved occupations' by which exemption from military service was granted according to the job they did rather than to which union they belonged.[9]

The introduction of conscription in 1917 was highly controversial for some on the left, especially the pacifists with its implications for conscientious objection. Clynes had always been strongly opposed to conscription and was critical of the tribunals set up to decide who should be conscripted, and to hear appeals for exemption. They were accused of taking men out of war production, and of browbeating conscientious objectors. He later wrote that 'nervous wrecks, semi-idiots and consumptives were forced by red faced presidents of tribunals to get into khaki and dragged out to die, cursing their country that had enslaved them in a military despotism they had been forced to swear loyalty.'10 This was unusual emotional language for him, and a reflection of depth of revulsion he felt for conscription, an indication of contradictions that did arise in the war between his patriotism and his conscience.10

The NUGGL continued to make informal approaches to other unions during the war with a view to eventual amalgamation, although any successful fusion of the two big federations had to wait until hostilities ceased. But any individual union that was willing to negotiate a merger was welcomed by Thorne and Clynes, and they made several proposals for the complete merger of a number of unions, including the Dockworkers and the still independent Birmingham Gas Workers. The other powerful general union, the Workers Union, was doing the same thing although it was not in favour of complete amalgamation along federal lines.11

After a series of political intrigues, Asquith was succeeded by Lloyd George in December 1916. The new Prime Minister was supported by only a minority of Liberal MPs and entirely dependent the Tories. Lloyd George's inspiring oratory and energy seemed such a contrast to Asquith's apparent lethargy, but those Labour MPs willing to continue in the new coalition were open to charges of hypocrisy. Lloyd George was so keen to keep Labour on board that he offered better terms for its support, and these included state control of the mines and shipping, in addition to the introduction of food rationing. Although he disapproved of the way in which the Asquith coalition had been brought down, Clynes thought that the war situation was so serious that

Labour should give its full support and participate in the the new government.12

He admired the dynamism and energy of Lloyd George and, while being well aware of his faults, thought he would be a far more effective war leader. Arthur Henderson joined Lloyd George's five-man inner war cabinet. George Barnes was made Minister of Pensions, and among the junior appointments Clynes accepted the post of Parliamentary Secretary to Lord Rhondda, the Minister for Food Control. This made him effectively the main government spokesman on food matters in the House of Commons, and involved answering parliamentary questions and taking a leading role in debates.

Clynes had been a critic of government food policy for some time, and answered his critics for accepting his role in the new ministry by claiming he had the support of the trade unions and rank and file party members, but was still open to charge of inconsistency. At first the government had been opposed to any interference with the food market, and preferred a 'business as usual' policy. But by 1917 this had become impossible, with a danger of serious food shortages caused by German U-Boats sinking Allied merchant shipping. Arthur Henderson was sent on a special mission to Petrograd to try to get armed Russian support for the Allies, or at least some kind of arrangement to obtain the vast new food supplies that were needed.13

As the country had moved on to a stance of 'Total War' the government had adopted a more 'statist-corporatist' approach to the production and distribution of food and to the direction of labour. In the first two years of war, food shortages had been localized and of short duration and then, when higher prices provided an incentive to increase supplies, demand was satisfied. But as the war progressed, shortages and price inflation increased without apparent respite, and there was much more demand for state intervention. This had been a plea of Clynes for some time, and was given added impetus by industrial unrest caused by higher food prices, coupled with the suspicion of profiteering.14

When the post of Parliamentary Secretary's post was offered to Clynes he therefore felt obliged to accept, although he claimed he was not eager for preferment and had turned down previous approaches to serve. There was a genuine belief that he could help improve the situation and help to make the right policies. He believed in the strict control of the price and distribution of food on grounds of equity, efficiency, and as a means of reducing industrial unrest that could seriously disrupt the war effort. Another reason for taking up the post was that he felt the country needed Labour's help in dealing with a situation impinging so much on the living standard of the working classes.

The criticism of him for taking up the post continued, however, and among these was a rather pompous and threatening letter from the ILP, stating that 'in joining the government without having consulted or informed the National Council of the ILP or your ILP colleagues, your action is contrary to the obligation placed on you as a parliamentary nominee of the ILP.' Clynes replied that he had received the consent of his union executive, and backed by the branches in addition to his local Labour Party in North-East Manchester and the ILP's objections were not in the best interests of labour.15

The work was gruelling with fifteen hour days and seven day weeks, masses of detail and statistics to master, conferences to attend, and answering criticism in the House of Commons. The Minister for Food, David Alfred Thomas, was born in Aberdare and been a colliery company executive and company director. An ally of Lloyd George, he had been elected Liberal MP for Aberdare in 1888, then lost his seat at the 1910 election. He had been sent to the USA in 1914 to negotiate for the supply of munitions, and on his return was abroad the *Lusitania* with his daughter when it was torpedoed and sunk. They were fortunate to survive. Thomas was appointed to the Lords as Lord Rhondda by Lloyd George in 1917, and put in charge of the new food ministry.

Clynes came to admire the energy and single-minded focus of Rhonnda, and they worked well together from the outset. The key to their strategy for food supply was strict regulation, to ensure fair distribution and to minimise suffering. Clynes had to stave off demands for relaxing regulations from all kinds of people and organisations, representing both consumers and producers. The world wheat harvest had failed in 1916, and U-boats had sunk hundreds of ships carrying it across the Atlantic. Flour had to be strictly controlled, and wheaten flour had to be diluted as the crisis became more acute with shortages of maize, potatoes, and other commodities. The result was a un-appetising grey husk-filled sour bread which was naturally very unpopular. An order was issued by the ministry that bread less than a day old should still be sold, and 'fancy breads' prohibited. There were protests from both bakers and thousands of consumers sent in certificates showing they could not eat the 'War Bread' as it was called.16

One of the biggest problems arising from food shortages was deliberate profiteering, largely by middle-men and agents. An example was beans that rose to very high prices, with a consignment shipped at £36 a ton changing hands at three times the price, and ending up at a retail price of £95 a ton in 1917. The same thing occurred with butter, this time profits going to the City speculators. This infuriated Clynes, who saw the moral dimension of investors gambling on foodstuffs that the merchant seamen had risked their lives to bring to these shores, and also the way it led to increasing the price that some very poor households had to pay for their food.

There is no doubt that fortunes were made by these speculators in food and drink during the war, and in particular luxuries of all kinds in high demand which were not imported at all for the duration of war. They had often been bought in bulk in 1914 and released slowly on to the market during the war years as prices increased, the most lucrative being luxuries such as whisky and other spirits. In 1917, prices exceeded pre-war levels by 178% for sugar, 100% or bread, 153% for mutton, and over 100% for most other commodities. Almost everything was scarce, made worse by increasing losses of merchant shipping, with 50,000 tons of sugar alone lost in sunk shipping in 1917 alone. There was such an emergency shortage that a food mission was sent to New York with powers to purchase any type of meat, and as a result approximately £200 million worth of ham and bacon was purchased and shipped over.17

It had been decided to set up a Food Council to implement the central regulation of supplies, and consisted of Lord Rhondda, Clynes, and eight or nine civil servants from the ministry. They met three or four times a week to settle outstanding issues, co-ordinate policy, and respond quickly to an unstable situations that arose. It was quite effective and was able to act quickly to avoid excessive bureaucratic delay. It consulted widely, especially the Consumers Council, the creation of which had largely been Clynes' idea. The Consumers Council consisted of people with a wide knowledge and interest in food issues, drawn from producers, consumers, cooperative societies and other experts. It was often critical of government policy, but usually constructive and kept in close contact with local authorities food committees, consumers organisations, working men's clubs and so on.18

A vocal critic of the food policy was H.M. Hyndman, the revolutionary socialist founder of the SDP, and Clynes approached him to join the Consumers Council on which he proved combative and determined. He came up with some constructive ideas and, although he and Clynes had very different personalities and political beliefs, worked well together and developed a mutual regard. When the war ended Clynes felt British society owed Hyndman a debt, but they shared similar views on state honours, no doubt confirmed by the recent scandal over the sale of honours in which Lloyd George had been implicated. When the chair of the Consumers Council was given a knighthood after the war, Hyndman proposed a resolution that stated that honours were an abomination. Another of Hyndman's concerns was that British people should have priority, and he proposed another resolution that it was wrong to send food to foreign countries until all poor British people had enough to eat.[19]

The post was no sinecure, and Clynes was working long hours but the job was satisfying, helping to avert starvation for millions. Some of the regulations on food control seemed petty and restrictive, such as the ban on the throwing of rice at weddings or controlling the price of sweets, but they were intended to make clear that all citizens were responsible and needed to contribute to the national emergency. A woman found feeding her Pekingnese with rump steak was fined £20, as was a farmer feeding bread crusts to his pigs. These well-publicised examples at least showed that everyone was affected, as did the endless daily queues of pale looking women with their children outside grocers, bakers and butchers shops. They creeped slowly closer to the entrance of the shop, only to find often on reaching it that supplies had run out.[20]

There was a campaign on the Home Front to encourage food production, and not just among farmers. Everyone was encouraged to grow vegetables in their gardens, and Clynes was impressed to see that even the royal household at Windsor Castle was complying with food rationing. The immaculate lawns at Windsor were dug up and planted with vegetables, and on an official visit Mary Clynes found herself in the peculiar position of discussing the merits of different varieties of vegetables with Queen Mary![22]

There was also a concerted effort to ensure more allotments were producing food. In 1915 a Cultivation of Lands Order permitted a new wave of allotment cultivation throughout the country. To encourage this, further model plots were set up for demonstration purposes in parks, such as those in Kensington Gardens. Railway land was reclaimed for allotment cultivation, and the number of new applications for plots increased every year. By 1919 they were running at 7,000 a week.[23]

Eventually, it was possible to lower bread prices by 25% through government subsidies under a 'Bread First' policy, not least to avert any rising panic as food queues grew longer. This was a step towards a national food control policy, turning the state into the controller of the nation's food supply, effectively selling meat, bread and other necessities. This kind of trading state was supported with some reservations, and delegated to Clynes' overall supervision. It involved asking local authorities to organise Food Committees consisting of twelve members, including at least one woman to represent housewives, plus a representative of labour. There were also regional Food Committees to advise them, which had a legal staff to prosecute those who disobeyed the regulations. There were 7,000 prosecuted during the war years, of which 935 were successful, with fines of £420,000 collected. Clynes ordered all the local committees to work in co-operation with the women's consumer groups, co-operative societies and lay experts in devising plans for the distribution of food via retailers and wholesalers. It was felt particularly important to fix commodity prices in relation to supply, much to the anger of large speculators.24

In grasping the potential for state intervention in the economy, Clynes anticipated the demand management theory of John Maynard Keynes, who was already working in the Treasury. In 1917 at the Labour Party conference he proposed a resolution stating:

> The Government can, if it chooses, analyse the public works,
> and the orders of the National Departments and
> Local Authorities in such a way as to maintain aggregate
> demand for labour in the whole Kingdom (including that
> of capitalist employers) approximately at a uniform level
> from year to year; and it is therefore the first duty of
> the government to prevent any consideration or widespread
> fluctuations in the total numbers of employed in times of
> good or bad trade.25

This may have been too ambitious for the time, but it was adopted and stands as a sad 'might have been' compared with the orthodox Treasury view that was actually pursued in the 1920s, and especially during the crisis of 1929-31. But wartime conditions, with the need for the mobilisation of industry and maximisation of production, meant that it was seen as necessary to regulate aspects of the economy, both production and consumption, including food.

In July 1918 ration cards were introduced for sugar, butter, margarine, and lard. They showed the number of

people in each household and had detachable
counterfoils to be given to the shopkeeper. The amount
of food available per person was fixed, and regulated
with agreed suppliers. There were initial difficulties with
some people having problems understanding and using
their cards including, famously, Lloyd George. These
were followed by meat ration cards, even though the
meat on sale was often of poor quality, and included
horsemeat as a substitute for beef and mutton. Although
the supplies of some food products increased, and the
retail prices began to fall, the rationing schemes were
tightened up. The country was combed for beef supplies
and those available were quickly exhausted in about
two weeks, as no merchant ships were getting through
in the submarine-infested waters of the Atlantic. There
were reports of huge queues of 4,000 people forming at
2 am on freezing January mornings, at the Smithfield
wholesale meat market in London. The meat shortages
were followed by another bread shortage, and Clynes
had to reassure the House of Commons about the fear
of riots occurring in the country.26

The new level of state interference led to
the formation of a Socialist National Defence
Committee to promote socialist measures to aid the
war effort, and to oppose the pacifist elements in
the ILP. It included Robert Blatchford and A.M.
Thompson, now the editor of the *Clarion,* and also
supported by Ben Tillett, Henry Hodge, and H.M.
Hyndman. These patriotic socialists had support from
a few Tories, such as Alfred Milner and Arthur Steel-
Maitland, and changed into the British Workers League.

They wanted more economic controls, better wages, imperial free trade, opposition to conscientious objectors and any attempt to end hostilities. They wanted a fight to the finish with retaliatory sanctions against Germany after an all-out victory.

Even though a number of Labour MPs belonged to the BWL, Clynes kept his distance. He distrusted it after 1918 particularly when it began adopting candidates to stand against pacifist Labour MPs, such as Ramsay MacDonald at Leicester East. Although Clynes opposed his pacifist views, he respected conscientious objection and was no warmonger. He saw the actions of the BWL as damaging to the united labour movement, as he did also the ILP which was busy selecting candidates to stand against sitting Labour MPs who were pro-war such as George Barnes in Glasgow. In April 1917 Arthur Henderson resigned his Cabinet post after his plans to end the war early were rejected, and he was replaced as Labour leader by Willie Adamson while Clynes stayed at the Food Ministry.

There is good reason to see war time food policies, including price controls, as helping the calorie intake of the population. During the war the intake of calories was maintained, and the calorie gap between skilled and and unskilled workers closed. But the same did not apply to vitamins and foodstuffs not considered vital to health such as fresh fruit and vegetables, which were not regulated. When prices rose, consumption fell, as did the intake of vitamin C in particular. But war food policy did still manage to maintain an adequate and fairly balanced diet for most people, such as the 'Bread First' policy, and the closing of inequalities in this respect was a guide to what could be achieved in peacetime.[27]

In February 1918 Rhonnda received a request from the food authorities in the United States to stop all the brewing of all beer in Britain, together with the US, in order to conserve grain supplies. Clynes opposed this on the grounds that 'for the workmen beer is food, drink and recreation', arguing that most drank in moderation, and that public houses had a social significance in providing a place of release from crowded homes and domestic tension. A cartoon showed Clynes with a barrel of beer in one arm facing the well-known temperance campaigner, Leif Mills MP, who is holding a drawn dagger. Clynes is saying 'Through my heart first.' and the cartoon bears the caption 'Further Hostilities on the Home Front.'

The brewing industry was strongly in favour of the continued production, supported by most of the Tory MPs, although certainly not at the cost of further state control. A few, such as Arthur Steel Maitland, wanted to impose some controls to ensure the workers got their constant supply of beer. It was another example of the war bringing some Tories together with Labour people to promote the well-being of the working class even if it meant drastic market intervention. In doing so, they hoped to make a common front against the Liberals who were in favour of free market and trade, and which they hoped would have electoral advantages later.

At this advanced stage in the conflict large numbers of wounded and mutilated men were seen on the street, still in uniforms, as well as recovering in hospitals and in sanatoriums. Clynes was deeply affected when he saw them on the streets of London and Manchester, feeling that these men had suffered, and so many died, for a cause they did not fully comprehend and had been told it was their duty to support. It convinced him that the working men and their families needed more than ever a government formed from people of their own class, who would prevent a repetition of such as conflagration.

At the Food Ministry, the strain was telling on Lord Rhondda, and his doctors advised him to take an immediate rest for the sake of his life. But he decided to carry on as the food situation was still critical, and continued working 15 hour days with all his heavy responsibilities. He heart was weak, and got weaker, until in July 1918 he died. Clynes was devastated and attended the memorial service at St Margaret's Westminster. He was sitting behind Lloyd George who at the end of the service wrote something on the margin of a hymn sheet, tore it off, and passed it back to Clynes. It was an invitation to have lunch the next day. When he arrived at 10 Downing Street he found Lloyd George in a jubilant mood. They discussed the progress of the war, and went on to talk about the food situation. Lloyd George said that he wanted Clynes to take over Rhonnda's post as Controller of Food Policy, and despite some reservations he felt obliged to accept.28

Having first got the approval of his constituency party before accepting the post, Clynes made his first appearance as the Minister of Food in the House of Commons on July 17 1918, feeling rather self-conscious as he walked to his place on the front bench. Even at this late stage in the war, German submarines were a menace to merchant shipping and imported food supplies remained unstable. Clynes continued to work long hours, and late into the evenings at the Food Ministry, and on his way home some nights saw the crowds gathered in the underground platforms as he went to get his train home. There were thousands of terrified people trying to escape the German raids, rushing for the shelters with the children crying, shattered glass, fire engines and anti-aircraft lorries.29

The heavy workload at the Ministry continued right up to the end of the war, and involved a huge amount of correspondence for Clynes, routine administration and attending conferences. He also had to meet groups of businessmen, importers, dealers and merchants, and speak at large public meetings where thousands of hungry and angry people wanted to know what was happening to ease the situation. There was also the responsibility of keeping in touch with the food authorities of the Allies, and arranging exchange of food supplies. In addition to all this he had to make appearances in the House of Commons, contribute to debates, and answer questions on all aspects of food policy from backbench MP's, who were inundated with letters full of complaints from constituents. They were to continue right up to the end of the war as well as those about the regulation of supply, profiteering and black marketing, and he was often heckled and had to face considerable abuse.

Many of the letters he received were amusing, such as

one complaining about a shopkeeper in the Midlands. It made a request that the regulations be more strictly applied, but 'if sir, you take proceedings which this case is so well deserved, please do not reveal my name, because the shopkeeper is my mother in law.' In July 1918 Clynes travelled to Blackpool for a conference, and the delegates were given a fish tea on strict ration rationing lines. His piece of fish was minute and when he had eaten the tiny portion he asked the waitress for a second helping he was told 'I'm afraid I daren't. They say the Food Controller is present!'[30]

The war ended suddenly, and in the streets there were celebrations with complete strangers linking arms, and the clippies on the buses being kissed by their passengers. As Clynes made his way around the city he saw enormous bonfires lit in Trafalgar Square, Piccadilly Circus and elsewhere, with furniture, prams and old clothes were thrown on them. The victory had been hard won, but the peace could also have some nasty surprises in store, and Clynes was not too anxious to face them having enjoyed his time in the coalition government. He was gratified to have been useful in the war effort, helping to make conditions on the Home Front a bit more tolerable and equable.[31]

In a hushed House of Commons on 11 November 1918 the terms of the armistice were read out by the Prime Minister. Then, Lloyd George called a general celection, hoping to take advantage of his popularity as 'the man who won the war' while the atmosphere of patriotism still lingered. The time for a resumption of party politics had arrived, and Clynes in some ways regretted the end of the coalition. He admired Lloyd George and others who had served in the wartime government, and had impressed by their commitment to the people and the national interest. The participation of the Labour Party in the coalition, however controversial initially, was to its longer-term benefit. The work of Clynes and his Labour colleagues in the government from 1916 increased the prestige of the Labour leadership and enabled them to share some of the reflected popularity of victory. Clynes was fortunate being involved in the implementing of planning and state regulation policy, of which he approved and did not conflict with his conscience. He had seen how the machinery of the state could be mobilised for the benefit of all the people in wartime, seeing no reason why it could not continue in peacetime.

6
Breaking Through

The patriotic atmosphere, not least among the working class, carried over into the election campaign. Labour could hope to benefit from this, having put aside party rivalry and contributed to the war effort in the wartime government. In doing so they also managed to exert influence in promoting and protecting the interests of the working class on the home front, in which Clynes had played an important role. In addition, though organisations like the Emergency Workers National Committee, pressure had been brought on ministers and civil servants on a range of working class concerns from wages to food policy. This body had close links with the Labour Party, and kept Clynes well aware of food and cost of living issues. During the war the expected industrial militancy failed to materialise and strike activity was negligible, although there was still discontent that carried over to the peace. The unrest showed itself almost immediately and the number of strikes in 1918 started to rise.

An outstanding grievance remained war profiteering, as Clynes was only too well aware, especially when it was coupled with the casualties and huge sacrifices that had taken place. He knew of these concerns through his trade union connections, and did what he could with food policy and rationing to placate their anger. The rent price restrictions, and the wage rises helped control this discontent during the war, but it was always likely to out after the peace when these when these were lifted. It was partly this that made Clynes reluctant to see the coalition government break up, although he realised that its continuance could only be temporary.

However, the tactics of Lloyd George put the Labour Party on the defensive with his election slogan of 'a Land fit for heroes to live in'. It created the impression that Labour wanted to let the Germans off lightly while the coalition Liberals and their Tory allies wanted to squeeze them dry. Before the campaign started, Labour held a special conference to decide policy, and several delegates demanded an immediate withdrawal from the coalition government on the grounds that Lloyd George had broken the political truce. Clynes spoke against this, arguing that Labour was now the only moderating influence in the country, and was duty bound to remain within the government for the time being, no matter what the political cost. It could exercise restraint on the drafting of peace terms and ensure economic fairness for a transitionary period. He was also convinced that without working class representation in government there was likely to be another war in his lifetime.[1]

The opposition to staying in the coalition government was led by the Fabians, and a party conference majority supported breaking away to fight the election in a clear opposition to other parties. The *NewStatesman*, then quite influential, also strongly opposed Labour continuing in the coalition, and Sydney Webb encouraged Henderson to stand again for the leadership against any coalition minister who might do so. He called on Labour to withdraw from 'an outdated party truce', and he and Beatrice Webb's view was that even if Labour only got around 60 seats at the election, it was important it stood alone as the official opposition to the Liberal-Conservative government.

The 1918 conference was also notable for the adoption by Labour of a new constitution that included Clause IV, a pledge to nationalise the commanding heights of the economy. It also opened up the party to wider trade union participation, expanding the membership of the National Executive Committee to include eleven trade unionists out of a total of twenty three members. The NEC was to be chosen at the annual conference which gave the trade unions much more power. Clynes welcomed both changes, although there was opposition from MacDonald and others on the grounds that it was leading to a trade union tyranny.2 But to Clynes, the unions were the most important element in the labour movement, and this should be reflected in the party policy making structure. It is also doubtful if the trade unions would have accepted the socialist policy inherent in Clause IV if they were not given more power in the party. But the ILP in particular were still unhappy about the increase in trade union influence, and also by the reduction of its own influence by the decision to set up individual constituency Labour Parties with individual party membership lists.

Once the decision to come out of the coalition government had been made, Clynes resigned from the government with the other Labour ministers, with the exception of George Barnes who refused to resign and was duly expelled from the Party. The division of the Liberals gave some hope to Labour that it would be able to make an electoral breakthrough, fighting on a broader front contesting far more seats without having to concern itself with an electoral partners It had previously contested no more than seventy-eight seats, but in 1918 it fought in 388 constituencies. It was also counting on gathering votes from the enlarged electorate, as the vote had now been extended to males voters over the age of 21 and to women over the age of 30, in recognition of their contribution to the war effort.

Lloyd George and the coalition Liberals were fighting in alliance with the Tories, plus twenty-eight candidates of the National Democratic and Labour Party. This had had been formed by Barnes and the National Workers League among others. A coupon of approval was given by Bonar Law, the Tory leader, to all Liberal and NDP coalition candidates to assure them they would not be opposed by official Conservative candidates. During the so-called 'Coupon Election' of 1918 the patriotic pro-war atmosphere remained high, as did the popularity of Lloyd George. They were unlikely to benefit the Labour Party, despite its supportive efforts in the war although it still managed to have 57 MPs elected. But this was not the breakthrough the party had hoped for, and several of its prominent figures were defeated including Snowden, Henderson and, most damagingly, MacDonald himself.

Clynes's constituency boundaries had changed, and he was re-elected for the slightly safer seat of Manchester Platting, but the outcome of the election was as a whole disappointing for Labour. But it did obtain 22% of the

vote which was an advance, and its fifty-seven MPs plus
four independent ILP MPs made it the official
Opposition. There were only 28 Asquithian Liberals, and
the Sinn Fein members refused to attend. But even
though Labour was the government in waiting it was
only a modest improvement over 1910, and the landslide
win of Lloyd George gave him a large majority. Some
some Labour candidates, such as J.H. Thomas in Derby,
took full advantage of the role of Labour in 'winning'
the war and played up their patriotic credentials to the
full, but this would not work so well in Manchester. The
new male voters, including demobbed servicemen, did
not turn to Labour in large numbers and together with
the new women voters seemed mainly concerned that
Germany paid dearly for its defeat.

When Parliament reassembled in January 1919 the
absence of MacDonald meant a new leader was needed,
and William Adamson was elected with Clynes chosen
as vice Chairman, essentially deputy Leader. But it was
difficult to build up an effective momentum as the
Opposition, with little room for initial manoeuvre, and
with support for the Versailles settlement having almost
no dissent. They missed the tactical skills of Ramsay
MacDonald and his leadership stature while, in exile, he
complained bitterly about the quality of the new leadership, allegingthat they 'had tasted the fleshpots' and so
implying they had no taste for confrontation.3

Clynes was now free to involve himself again in trade
union work and Labour Party matters, and tried to inject
some energy into a campaign for a fairer distribution of

war profits. He argued that the 'total reserve of private wealth among the richer classes in Britain during the war years has been increased by something over £3,000,000,000. This enormous private gain was accrued at a time when the debt of the state had increased by £6,000,000,000.' The Excess Profits Tax of 1918 only collected £1,000,000,000 leaving the huge sum of £2,000,000,000 in pockets of wartime profiteers, and he demanded that it be collected and used to defray war debts, in effect a capital levy. This was an effort to embarrass the coalition government, some of whose members looked rather like those characterised by Stanley Baldwin as 'hard-faced men who looked as if they had done well out of the war' and to play on popular feeling that many had done so.4

Almost immediately the war was over there were serious problems with demobilization. The returning soldiers had been promised when they joined up that there would be jobs waiting for them, but they found these promises were worth very little in peacetime. At first the government's plan was to release the skilled and those with managerial backgrounds first into the labour market, but this created huge discontent. They had also been the last to be called up, and were now the first to be de-mobbed. There were demonstrations, and 3,000 men even occupied Horse Guards Parade in protest. When the 'first in first out' principle was adopted by Churchill as Secretary of War, over 4 million were then demobilized. Although a short-lived post-war industrial boom absorbed many of these, many others had difficulty finding employment. In towns and cities there ex-soldiers were to be seen on street corners, still wearing their 'British warms' as they waited in queues or hung about on street corners.5

As Clynes made his way to the House of Commons each day, these men on the streets were a constant reminder of the futility and stupidity of war. In Manchester, as in other industrial cities, thousands of young working class men had answered the call to join up in 1918, but there hopes of a reciprocal generosity and gratitude by the government was not forthcoming. The conditions the survivors faced were worse in many cases than before they went away to fight, and although the violence authorities feared did not materialise, the anger was palpable. When Clynes spoke at a public meeting at Belle Vue in Manchester on 1st May 1919 he received a very hostile reception. Despite being by now something of a local hero, and a possible future Labour leader, sections of the angry crowd shouted him down and he must have regretted accepting the invitation to speak. He was booed by two groups in particular in the crowd: the more radical trade unionists and Irish supporters of independence. The former were angry about high unemployment while the latter were protesting about Labour policy on Ireland – supporting Home Rule in principle while stopping short of endorsing its full implications.6

In the summer of 1919 Clynes travelled to Oxford to receive an an honorary Doctor of Commercial Laws degree, and sat through the ceremony in the Sheldonian conducted in Latin, listening to the eulogies. As he could understand none of it, it provided 'a very humane means of conferring a valued academic distinction, without raising too many blushes on the cheeks of the recipient' He was in the company of Field Marshall Earl Haig, Lord Beatty and Marshal Joffre, all military contributors to the war effort, which might have made him feel rather uncomfortable. But he found the experience interesting and poignant, in contrast to his own studies amid the whirling machinery in the Oldham mill and by candle light at home. And yet fate had 'brought me now to stand, in a scarlet gown, in the oldest home of British learning', he had begun to see his own private history as an allegory of what might be possible for millions of others. He had been a pathfinder, but the struggle and vagaries of fate that consigned him to an early life of poverty and ignorance should not be a barrier for all those who came after.7

The small band of Labour MPs who sat on the Opposition benches seemed a rather depleted group, faced with the massed ranks of the Liberal Coalitionist and Conservative MPs. Most of them were elderly trade unionists, including twenty-five miners. They were a rather uninspiring bunch and even more right-wing than the pre-war parliamentary party. Some local   party activists began to see the parliamentary party as irrelevant in such a situation, and began to turn towards ideas of 'direct action.' As unemployment rose once the short post-war boom ended, food was 115% over 1914 prices and worker dissatisfaction showed itself in a new preparedness to take strike action. In this more militant atmosphere syndicalist ideas became popular, based on a 'Triple Alliance' of miners, railwaymen and transport workers, and aiming ultimately at a general strike. There was a massive strike in Glasgow and 12,000 troops were called out with six tanks and machine gunnests set up, a huge over-reaction by the government. There were also strikes of textile workers in Lancashire, and in London even the policemen went on strike for its trade union to be recognised

All this alarmed the Labour Party, even though it was its ineffectiveness that partially persuaded the strikers to take on the government head-on. The timid Adamson was re-elected leader by the rest of the trade union MP's, and they agreed with Clynes that a general strike would do considerable harm to the labour movement, and cause hardship to thousands of families without necessarily leading to a favourable settlement. Like the other moderate union leaders Clynes never believed in provoking strikes, and that 'strikes like wars cause losses to both sides', never to be used without the gravest cause.8

The NUGGL leadership believed that the ballot box should always be the means of achieving social and political change, with Clynes arguing this case forcibly at the 1920 Union conference:

' ...the new doctrine (of direct action) is preached with a child-like belief in its success as a method for economic reconstruction. We cannot show the failure of political efforts which have never been fully tried at all. Working class electoral power has only recently become overwhelming, and the means to use that power had only been offered to the workers in the past few years in the form of a well-established national party.9

In his view direct action would damage the prospects of a Labour government, and threaten to destroy the unity that the labour movement had so recently built up.

After the war the NUGGL under Thorne and Clynes, who was now the elected President, continued to push for further amalgamation. Their first proposals were to the Dockworkers Union, but a ballot held by its members in 1919 had a majority against, encouraged by their powerful National Organiser, Ernest Bevin. The NUGGL was disappointed after the energy and time expended on the negotiations, but other merger plans proved more successful in these early post-years. The Birmingham Gas Workers finally agreed to a merge as did the Federation of Women Workers in 1920. This had over 40,000 members under its leader, the formidable Margaret Bondfield, and obtained some generous terms that included the creation of a Women's Department, a Women's National Committee, and the appointment of a Chief Women's Staff Officer. These developments, and the influential role that Bondfield came to play as both an MP and member of the TUC General Council, made that the union came to enjoy the reputation as the union for women workers.

Clynes was more than ever convinced of the benefits of union amalgamating, especially as the skilled workers were doing the same, and felt the unskilled should not be in a weaker position. He thought it was essential given their inherent weakness in negotiations, and would give greater strength at less cost while keeping the members subscriptions uniformly low. All members of an enlarged union could also enjoy common benefits irrespective of their location or employer. The friction of rivalry between unions would also be avoided, which allowed unscrupulous employers to divide and rule in negotiations on terms and conditions, and to withhold recognition of one union over another. The guiding sentiment followed by Clynes was that of 'unity in strength,' and whenever that principle was forgotten it was to the detriment of the labour movement as a whole. In January 1920 the other big federation of unskilled workers, the Workers Union, as well as the Municipal Employees Association and the National Associated Union of Labour (NAUL) started talks with the NUGGL towards amalgamation. If successful, it would have created the largest union in the country with 1,250,000 members.

However, the negotiations proved difficult with the two big general unions having different interests. Both had grown quickly during the war due to the expansion of the armaments industries, but the NUGGL had a third of its members in the public utilities and local government employment, while the Workers Union were stronger in the private sector engineering industries. It was badly affected by the post-war slump, especially as it carried a larger administrative staff than the NUGGL, with a hundred officials. The latter only employed sixty, although that did not include full-time branch secretaries. This smaller headquarter's staff was an advantage when membership fell due to the rising unemployment, and running costs became an issue. But during times of economic and rising employment it could be a weakness. The NUGGL was always rather parsimonious when it came to expenditure, including both incurring costs before membership had risen, and in the parsimonious benefits paid. This was again in contrast to the Workers Union which had a more generous benefits scheme which, given the number of disputes and stoppages it was involved in, also became a weakness.10

The weaknesses of the Workers Union were revealed during economic downturn in 1920-21 when its membership halved to 247,000, and nearly all its cash reserves were used up. The NUGGL had also suffered with a falling membership, but by the end of 1921 it still had 356,000 paid-up members and emerged from the crisis as the stronger of the two big general unions. This encouraged further negotiations or amalgamation, but there were still sticking points about voting procedures, and who should lead the new enlarged union. The talks broke down again over this and other issues such as the level of benefit payments for members on strike, on the union's relations with MPs and on its organisation and structure. However, negotiations with the smaller unions - the National Amalgamated Union of Labour and the Municipal Employees Association continued with more success, although it was not until 1924 that a newer enlarged union was formed which became the General Municipal WorkersUnion (GMWU) with Thorne as the General Secretary and with Clynes as President. The

Worker's Union eventually went on to merge with the dockers to form the Transport and General Workers Union in 1928.

In the spring of 1921 a proposed general strike day was set for the 15 April, and the government made great play of what it called labours 'menace to the state'. An emergency force of several hundred thousand citizen soldiers were mobilised from the middle classes, and given rifles, bayonets and machine guns. Then tanks and armoured cars appeared in London and elsewhere with regular troops in tin hats and full war kit parading in the streets. Hyde Park was closed and designated as a milk distribution centre with hundreds of big army bell tents, while Regents Park and Kensington Gardens were filled with army huts. It looked as if the government expected an imminent revolution or at least a civil war.

Clynes was pleading the case of the miners in the House of Commons on the day that the railwaymen and transport workers withdrew their intention to strike, leaving the miners in the lurch. He was able to incorporate the news of this in his speech, and there followed wild cheering from the benches, not all of them from the government side opposite. Instead of seeing it as a regrettable defeat for labour, Clynes rather characteristically saw the cheering as a sign of 'how deep had been the uneasiness of members as to the outcome of the threatened struggle between three great unions and the government armed citizens regiments.'11

Perhaps unsurprisingly he was attacked as a traitor for this speech by many supporters of the strike, especially as he went on to say that had a ballot been held before 'Black Friday' a majority of workers would have voted against the strike.

After the collapse of the Triple Alliance there were less strikes and the parliamentary Labour Party felt more secure with the passing of the threat of direct action. Instead of seeing the collapse of the militancy as the result of intimidation and force, Clynes again typically saw it as evidence of the essential moderation, loyalty and common sense of the working class. He saw the Labour Party as reflecting these values and that as 'the Labour Party has grown in power, the menace of revolution has dwindled.,' so the party was the necessary bulwark to stave of the threat of revolution and violence. The party was indeed attracting more support, and won several by-elections as the Lloyd George coalition was becoming more divided and unpopular. Willie Adamson, feeling the pressure of events, resigned as Labour leader and Clynes was elected in his place.

It was a crucial time as he had to prepare and lead the party into the next general election, which was imminent. Despite the problems over his pro-war stance and willingness to serve in the wartime coalition, Clynes was generally respected and even held in affection by the majority of the parliamentary party, still heavily biased towards moderate trade unionists. Although lacking MacDonald's voice, dramatic projection and romantic rhetoric, Clynes was seen as the best available leader. He may have been physically unimpressive, small and slight, and lacking in charisma but projected a sense of purpose and dedication behind his quiet demeanour. And he did give the Labour Party administrative order, and brought the trade unions firmly onto the side of the leadership, establishing close links between the PLP, NEC and the TUC. But his qualities of quiet amiability and political shrewdness were not sufficiently inspiring for most of the party. Never an emotional speaker, his tone was generally emollient and courteous in debate, but that made his stinging barbs and sarcasm the more effective when they were employed, and he projected an overall sense of moral authority.

As leader of the PLP, Clynes found he had to devote a large amount of time to parliamentary business for five days a week, often having to remain in the House until a late hour, occasionally all night. There were constant speeches to be made from the Front Bench, chairing of party committees, attending conferences, demonstrations and other public meetings. There was also the routine of administrative work and of partymanagement, which was tiring and time-consuming, with few of the resources and staff available to a party leader to-day. And then the most important unofficial functions of any party leader, trying to keep colleagues with various shades of opinion together, took up time and energy in order to provide a unified to be more effective in parliamentary strategy.

In the face of rising unemployment the coalition government seemed to offer no answers, and Labour's popularity had increased as a result both at the local and national levels. It had been making considerable strides in local government and in the 1920's gained control in several large municipal authorities, including many London boroughs. This local power base became increasingly important, helping to define Labour's function and programme and giving executive experience to many talented young men such as Clement Attlee and Herbert Morrison. In boroughs such as Hackney, Bermondsey, Stepney and Poplar, Labour built an effective grassroots organisation, and did its best to improve housing and living conditions. Campaigns such that led by George Lansbury at Poplar in 1921 against a heavy unfair rate increase resulted in the imprisonment of local councillors and considerable publicity.

Most of the post-war unemployment was in the old basic industries, and it became a highly emotive issue for Labour. In September 1921 a couple of Labour MPs, one of whom was Will Thorne, were ordered by the Speaker to leave the House after they had accused MPs on the government benches of being 'political tricksters' and of gaining 'a victory over starving children' with its lack of an effective policy. Clynes then led the whole Labour group out of the Commons in protest, although typically he thought 'our absence served us no better than our presence.' But it made him very angry to hear coalition MPs, who had never known hunger or unemployment coldly dismiss Labour's proposals for relief.

The high unemployment reduced government revenue and, with a balanced budget always in mind, the demand for public expenditure reductions mounted. The orthodox view of the time was that taxation hindered investment, demand and economic growth. Any direct intervention in the economy during peacetime was not acceptable to the Conservatives who were dominant in the government, and controlled Lloyd George who had little room to maneouvre. His unpopularity grew by the month and strengthened Labour's appeal to the working class voters. The industrial troubles spread to the coal mines, docks, and transport, while the Irish civil war put more pressure on the government.

The end of the coalition government came when the Conservatives withdrew support from Lloyd George. He resigned to be succeeded by Bonar Law. An election was called in November 1922, and Labour was confident of doing much better this time. Clynes saw there was more enthusiasm for the party in Manchester, including in his own constituency of Platting where groups of children suddenly appeared during election campaign with dust-lids as cymbals, carrying banners and wearing Labour rosettes, marching through the streets canvassing. They became known as 'Clynes' Band', and for many years afterwards similar groups would turn out to support him at elections with banging drums, colours flying and urging people to 'VOTE FOR CLYNES'. This time he had no doubt he would win and the majority was comfortable.[12]

As the effective leader of the Party, Clynes had also to speak at meetings in other parts of the country and his speeches were more widely reported. This higher profile no doubt helped him to retain his own seat with an increased majority. The campaign of 1922 saw Liberal divisions continue, and many more Labour gains. After his own count was declared, Clynes watched the other results in the country being displayed along an illuminated sign in the middle of Manchester. He saw many 'Labour Gain' flash by, and it was soon clear the party had done well. The final result saw it double its share of the vote popular vote over 1918 with 29.65%, with a gain of 67 seats to bring its total to 142. This was a great success, given that nobody seriously thought the party was likely to achieve power. The Conservatives had 344 MPs, the Liberals 62 and the National Liberal 53 MPs. Of Labour members, thirty were from Scotland and thirty-two from the ILP which shifted the party leftwards in composition Many new talented people entered parliament for the time first time including Clement Attlee and Sydney Webb with a significant group of Clydeside MPs, most notably John Wheatley, James Maxton, and David Kirkwood. There were also ex-Liberal recruits to Labour such as Charles Trevelyan and Noel Buxton which gave a social leavening to the party. The social mix and background of Labour MPs was in any case now changing, with more from the middle-class occupations and backgrounds.

When the new parliament assembled, Clynes got off to an unfortunate start by failing to secure exclusive use of the Opposition Front Bench for Labour. It had to be shared with the Liberals, although in debates precedence would be granted to Labour as the largest of the non-Government parties therefore had to be recognized as the the 'official' Opposition with seats directly opposite the government front bench, and it was given four of the five so-called supply days for debates. At the first meeting of thePLP the most pressing issue was the election of a new party chairman or 'leader' as he was soon as be officially called. The vote was extremely close, and MacDonald by the narrow margin of only five votes. Clynes was to later claim he was told by some supporters that they were so sure of his victory they do not bother to vote.13 Whether this was true or not, MacDonald was not that with all his colleagues, and Clynes was given the credit for leading the party successfully during the election, and was held in considerable affection and respect. But the leadership performance in the House of Commons since 1918 had not been inspiring, and MacDonald was not associated this and offered a fresh start.

During his years of absence from Parliament, MacDonald had constantly sniped from the sidelines at what he called the party's 'lamentable weakness,' and even criticised it for playing the parliamentary game which he claimed made it a tool of capitalism. Despite playing the parliamentary 'game' so effectively himself before 1914, his post-1918 criticisms appeared to make him seem more radical than he actually was or intended to be, a talent that MacDonald was adept at employing when circumstances required. Neither was his criticism of Labour's performance entirely fair, and even the cautious Clynes was occasionally willing to lead dramatic protests in the Chamber, although generally he thought such methods were futile.

Clynes considered that he lost the leadership election because the left wing group of MPs, particularly those in the Clydeside group, 'demanded more demonstrations in the Commons than I was prepared to approve.'13 At the PLP meeting held before the ballot, MacDonald implied he would fight harder than Clynes had to get the ruling changed on Labour's sharing of the Opposition Front Bench, and would pursue and provide a vigorous radical opposition. Later, Clynes claimed that he felt relieved at having the burden of leadership lifted from him, but he must have been somewhat disappointed at having lost the chance to become the first Labour Prime Minister, having been in a leading position. In a later account Kirkwood, one of the newly elected Clydeside MP's, described the scene at the momentous meeting:

> On the left side sat the men who supported Mr Clynes of the General Worker's Union, Food Controller in 1918, and chairman of the Labour Party in the House of Commons in 1921-1922. With him were the trade union members. Nature had dealt unevenly with these men. She had endowed MacDonald with a magnificent presence, a full resonant voice, and a splendid dignity. Clynes was small, unassuming, of uneven features, and a voice without colour. There they sat: Clynes at ease and indifferent; MacDonald with his head in his hands, looking anxious and ill. Wehn the votes were counted, MacDonald was elected by a narrow majority. The Clyde men had supported him solidly. The result acted like magic on MacDonald. He sat up at once. All the lassitude and illness disappeared. He was as vigorousas any man in the room. John Wheatley looked at me and shrugged his shoulders. His uneasiness was growing. Clynes never turned a hair. 14

Later that day there was a meeting at the Kingsway Hall in Holborn organized by the party to welcome the new leader, but MacDonald did not turn up and Clynes had to step in to make the main speech, full of appeals for unity and loyalty. His personal ambition, as always, was tempered by the overriding need to keep the party and the movement, of which it was a part, united. He was always loyal, and considered himself the servant of the movement and would abide by whatever it decided was in the interest of the Labour Party. However much he disagreed with colleagues over strategy or policy he was always looking for some consensus and agreement. He never saw himself as more important than the party which was more than could be said for MacDonald whose vanity and personal ambition ultimately led to his departure. However, most of the new intake of Labour MPs opted for MacDonald simply because he seemed to the more attractive figure, and more likely to lead them to electoral success.

But the narrow failure of Clynes in the leadership election provides one of the fascinating 'what-ifs' of political history. The personal weaknesses and failings of MacDonald contributed to the collapse of the second Labour government, and the years in the wilderness for the party that followed. It is unlikely that Clynes or any other leader would have been willing, or even able to challenge the deeply entrenched economic orthodoxy of the time. But he was aware from wartime experience of the potential for the mass mobilisation of resources by the state, and its ability to influence demand and supply. But, as Prime Minister he would have faced the same pressures as MacDonald from the Treasury, City and business interests. But he would have done his best to have avoided a split in the party, having spent his life trying to maintain unity. He was unlikely to have gone ahead with cuts in unemployment benefit which might have delayed the general election, and possibly Labour's disastrous defeat.

Many of the new Labour MPs, including some of the 'Red' Clydesiders, were soon enveloped by the clubbable atmosphere of the House of Common. They were pleasantly surprised at the friendliness and affability of many Tories and Liberals, and the polite hearing they received even when proclaiming their socialist message. If this was the 'parliamentary embrace', from about 1922 several leading Labour figures were noticed attending social events and royal functions which came to be called the 'aristocratic embrace.'15 The wives of Labour MPs who had moved to London with their families, as Mary Clynes had done, tended to be socially isolated and the chance to attend social events were no doubt welcome. Mary Clynes was a very down-to-earth lady and no social climber unlike, for example, Mrs Snowden. Beatrice Webb who had realised the problem organised a series of lunches for the wives of Labour MPs at the Half Moon Club in Soho to bring them together, and help break down their social isolation.

In 1922 Clynes was sharply criticised for attending the marriage of Princess Mary, only daughter of King George V, but he considered the invitation as an honour for the Labour Party and a sign of its newly won respect. He put the case that 'the vast majority of Labour voters throughout Great Britain would like to be represented at a wedding to which they obviously offered their good wishes.14 This might sound rather disingenuous, but the there is no reason to doubt his sincerity, and it was in line with his general thinking. The Labour Party that its leaders, he believed, had a duty to act as representatives of the people on all official occasions whether they were to the personal liking of the person concerned or not. Clynes actually rather disapproved of a lot of the social and ceremonial side of political life and public office, including ceremonial dress, the frequent royal audiences and the other formal official engagements he later had to attend.

The Conservative government under Bonar Law, and then from 1923 under Stanley Baldwin, enjoyed a large majority. But Labour had now come of age and, as the main opposition party and felt more confident asserting itself. The King's Speech in 1923 had nothing to say about unemployment and, in the debate that followed, MacDonald castigated the dole, and outlined Labour's policy proposals for nationalising major industry and for a capital levy. He went further with the proposition that every privately owned property worth more than £5,000 should write down a proportion as belonging to the state which could be used to offset the National Debt.

As an industrialist, Stanley Baldwin sympathized with protective tariffs and a move away from free trade. With Neville Chamberlain as his Chancellor of the Exchequer, they wanted radical changes to economic policy. The need for a vote of confidence led to a general election being called in December 1923. This was a grave miscalculation as it united both sections of the Liberals and Labour in campaigning for the maintenance of free trade to prevent inflation and the lowering of workers living standards. The problem of unemployment was the other main issue as it had reached 8%, and the election was fought in an atmosphere of considerable bitterness among the unemployed, especially the miners and textile workers.

The outcome was 258 seats for the Conservatives, 158 for the two groups of Liberals and 191 for Labour. The Conservatives had lost their overall majority, Baldwin resigned and the King called the Labour leaders to Buckingham Palace. MacDonald, Henderson, Clynes and J.H. Thomas went along for the royal audience. As they stood waiting, Clynes marvelled at the turn of fate that had brought these of men of humble working class backgrounds, a clerk, a foundry worker, an engine driver and a mill-hand, to such august surroundings. He was not overawed by the gold and crimson plush, but was well aware of its historical significance, and felt that they were making history.

The King soon put them at their ease but seemed rather anxious, perhaps worried about what was in store for the country, and he did not hesitate to offer advice. He told them that the future of 'my people, and their whole happiness is in your hands, gentlemen. They depend upon your prudence and sagacity'.16 The shock of Labour in power, albeit as a minority government, led to alarmist scare mongering in the right-wing press and warnings of a Soviet or communist takeover. In the strongly monarchical society of the time, the confidence in Labour expressed by George V, whatever his own private reservations, may have had some importance in helping to legitimise the party as a government in the eyes of the public. Clynes thought so, and was deeply impressed by the King's behaviour, although he hardly had any choice as a constitutional monarch. To have shown antagonism or opposition to the elected government, however fragile its grip on power, would have been even more controversial and created a crisis.

7
Labour Troubles

The prospect of a Labour government created a shock and even panic in some sectors, exaggerated and exploited by the Tory Party and the right-wing press. The old fears of a communist take-over were revived, and dire warnings and forecasts made about what awaited the country. All these fears were, of course, alarmist and entirely groundless. The new Labour administration was in any case extremely weak, in a minority and entirely dependent on the Liberals for survival.

The government was, therefore, in no position to introduce radical change of any kind, never mind of a revolutionary nature. It was more likely, as Clynes pointed out in regard to Labour's enemies in the City, that they were '...not afraid we shall fail in relation to them. They are afraid that we shall succeed.'1 The huge propaganda fear campaign in the Rothermere press was more about the prospect of a Labour government itself and what it signified rather than what it might actually have been able to do. Labour had now breached the barrier and was 'inside the gate', and had to now be regarded as a serious party of power, to the chagrin of the established order.

When MacDonald came to form his government he faced some difficulties, notably the problem of who to include in his cabinet. This is always a tricky problem for an incoming Prime Minister, but in 1922 it was more so because by the lack of ministerial experience in the parliamentary party, apart from the few who had served in the wartime coalition government. MacDonald himself lacked any experience of government, and only Clynes and Henderson had cabinet experience. So, despite being exceptional in having experience as a minister, it was with some surprise that Clynes was not given a more important post than Lord Privy Seal, although he was also confirmed as Deputy Prime Minister.

The Clynes family also moved into No 11 Downing Street including Mary, their daughter Mabel and son Jack, who was now acting as secretary to his father. In order to find out what the duties of the post involved as he had no idea, Clynes went to see Lord Cecil, a Tory previous holder. To his surprise he was informed that it was largely ceremonial and carried hardly any serious responsibilities at all, in effect a sinecure with a salary attached. This made him even more displeased with the Prime Minister who had appointed him to the cabinet without any important responsibilities or powers.

The appointment may have been intended to keep a rival for the leadership in an uninfluential and obscure role. It may also have been intended to keep a leading trade unionist out of one of the main cabinet posts, or to allow Clynes to spend most of his time on the duties of deputy leader of the party. It was probably a mixture of all three, and the residence at No 11 Downing Street would give easy access to the prime minister and the cabinet next door. MacDonald exercised his charm and persuasiveness on Clynes, who would cause a row. But the feeling persisted that an ex-party leader with cabinet experience he should have been given a more important role.

As MacDonald had also reserved for himself the post of Foreign Secretary it meant that he would be away overseas a good deal, and the burden of leading the government in the House would fall on to the shoulders of Clynes. This would make for fifteen hour days and a huge burden of work, for which Clynes felt largely under-rewarded. Again, he made no public complaint about this, as always the party loyalist and even in private largely acceded to MacDonalds persuasiveness and did not push his displeasure too far. He no doubt felt flattered being consulted by MacDonald over the other cabinet appointments, which were extremely difficult to fill.

The unpreparedness of Labour for office was revealed when nobody in the party apparently knew all the posts that needed to be filled to form a complete government. They had a good deal civil service advice before the election, but the the result was such a surprise that party officials had to consult *Whitakers Almanack* to find all the junior posts that needed to be filled.2 Inevitably, the first Labour cabinet was extremely inexperienced, and several ministers had to be appointed from outside the party ranks. This was a worry to MacDonald, concerned that the new ministers might not be able to stand-up to their senior civil servants. He appointed quite a few right-wing trade unionists, excluded George Lansbury and appointed only two left-wingers, which again created resentment Most of the Labour's old campaigners were rewarded with some kind of post, and Philip Snowden appointed as Chancellor of the Exchequer with Arthur Henderson as Home Secretary.

There were a number of ex-Liberals in the administration and even two ex-Conservative peers were appointed, much to the outrage of many Labour members. MacDonald's friend, and golfing partner, C.B. Thompson, was made Air Minister. The motives behind MacDonald's appointments were to stop anyone in the government rocking the boat or causing problems, plus a a desire to present a respectable front to the established order and scupper any further charges that it was an administration sympathetic to revolutionary communism. This excessive caution was unnecessary as there was a certain amount of goodwill towards the new government among moderates in all parties, and no amount of placating would still the right wing press from taking every opportunity to denigrate the Labour Party and the government.

The post of Lord Privy Seal may have been largely ceremonial and with little power, but it was an ancient one, and it took Clynes into a world of precedence and tradition that the old order took extremely seriously. He learnt to his amusement that the office gave him precedence over all the dukes of the UK for official purposes, and his presence was required at many ceremonial and royal occasions, often to his irritation. This flim-flummery started with a visit to Windsor Castle with the rest of the cabinet to receive their seals office all dressed up in morning suits. On returning to Downing Street Clynes put his seal in his office safe, and it stayed

until he had to return it a few months later when he left
the post. They had only moved into 11 Downing Street
a few days earlier, and Mary's first comment on seeing
inside was that it lacked both a piano and a sewing
machine! The main reception room had such a weak
floor that it to be propped up from the kitchen below
to withstand the weight, while the general state of the
decoration was poor and rather neglected.3

Clynes continued to be frustrated by the amount of
court dress, etiquette and orders of precedence for all
official occasions at which he had to be present. These
included formal receptions, dinners and other occasions
of all kinds involving visiting heads of state and newly
appointed ambassadors. He saw all the dressing up in
court and ceremonial attire as serving no useful purpose
whatever, and thought it should be discontinued. In the
brief time in office he had no chance of achieving this,
so had to go along with the practice. He could have refused to conform, as some subsequent Labour ministers
ministers did, and dress in ordinary clothes on these
occasions but it was not in his nature to rebel. In any
case, MacDonald expected strict adherence to the letter
of precedence in all matters, including wearing correct
ceremonial dress, and King George V was also a stickler
for correct dress on all occasions. The court and formal
clothes may have flattered the tall distinguished looking
MacDonald, but the diminutive and ordinary looking
Clynes felt embarrassed dressed in top hats and tails. In
the end he felt he had to comply with the wishes of the
prime minister, considering it not worth arguing over a
relatively trivial and symbolic issue at a time of such

political instability for the new government with so many other issues with which to contend.

In some ways Clynes showed contradictory tendencies, pulled one way and then another on various issues, and this probably led to his reputation for indecisiveness, particularly during the second Labour government. The issue of ceremonial court dress was, despite its triviality, an illustration of his contradictory tendencies. For despite his privately expressed disdain for morning coats, plumed hats and ceremonial swords, part of him was nevertheless proud to be part of this Ruritanian charade.

> I have seen an ex-docker and ex-policeman Labour MPs turned into correctly dressed officials at Buckingham Palace, looking very much more distinguished and perfecting their bearing than certain immature noblemen sent to court from very wealthy households!'4

Although ceremonial dress was absurd and inconvenient it was important to him that the representatives of the people should look just as distinguished in it as royal personages or aristocrats. Neither did it apparently seem to him to symbolise the old order that Labour might to subvert.

This first Labour Government was in fragile state, a minority dependent on Liberal support to survive. The Tory opposition took every opportunity to embarrass it and exploit its weakness. They even criticised Labour ministers for having the temerity to accept salaries, even though ministers in the previous Tory administration had done so, and they put down a motion in the House of Commons for there reduction. This was treated as a vote of confidence, and the Government survived by a few votes.

Clynes soon found the expense of being a minister hard to bear, literally so on discovering that he was personally responsible for the cost of maintaining his official residence in Downing Street. He also discovered that he also had to pay the salaries of the cleaning and catering staff out of his own pocket which came to £2000 a year, a very large amount for the time. After being being in residence for a time, he received a bill for £68.16.10 for fuel, electricity, and heating which he was personally expected to pay.

He also had to pay the cost of the food bills for all official dinners and receptions, as well as the catering costs for all other occasions which came to £67 amonth. When he had to attend Buckingham Palace, which as Lord Privy Seal was quite often, a chauffeur and foot-man were required to be in attendance, and their wages had to be paid by the minister. The Clynes family had to buy extra furniture because the place was so poorly furnished, as well as glass, cutlery and other essentials which were lacking. All of this had to be met from his salary of £5,000 as a Cabinet minister.5

The situation was harder to bear because Clynes saw most of the official receptions and banquets as a waste of time, such as the palace banquet to welcome the King and Queen of Rumania which was followed a few weeks later by the state visit of the King of Abyssinia. A rather more important responsibility of the Lord Privy Seal was coordinating the work of the different ministers to meet the common objectives of the government. When the

Prime Minister was absent Clynes became what he called the 'Aunt Sally' of the Cabinet, taking the brunt of Tory and Liberal criticisms hurled at him daily on the floor of the House of Commons, from Baldwin, Lloyd George, Asquith, Churchill and the serried ranks of Tory and Liberal MPs. He did not find this at all pleasant, and party political jousting was less congenial on the Front Bench than it had been on the backbenches. Many on his own side were critical, holding him partly responsible or what they saw as Labour's timidity or lack of resolve. MacDonald may have been a more effective point scorer in the House of Commons, but whoever was leading the party would have faced the same problem. At the first sign of any uncompromising socialist policy, the Liberals would have sided with the Conservatives to vote the government out of office. Under this constraint it was impossible for Labour to even attempt to implement its manifesto promises, such as nationalisation and the capital levy. It was also weakened by the argument that it did not have a legitimate mandate to do so, given the lack of an overall majority and minority of the popular vote.

The most important of the government's few reforms that it did manage to get passed was the Housing Act, introduced by the Minister of Health John Wheatley, one of the few left-wingers in a ministerial post. It was to speed up slum clearance and the building of new houses and gave direct financial help to local authorities for municipal house building. Clynes made a speech that was unusually impassioned the debate on the bill, in which he said that 'our prisons and our public lavatories are better built than the dwellings of millions of the poor. Many an ex-prisoner finds his roof less weather- and less comfortable than his cell in jail.'6

He knew from personal experience, as did most of his colleagues on the Labour benches, about the appalling housing conditions in which his constituents lived.These were usually dirty overcrowded, unhygienic, insanitary, and lacking in basic amenities. They had been a major factor of poverty in British cities for over a hundred and little had been done about it. What improvements there had been was left largely to the housing charities, and the act gave really substantial powers to the local councils for the first time. It set out a fifteen year programme of slum clearance and house building, to re-house people in decent accommodation and helping to boost the construction industry. But Philip Snowden, the Chancellor of the Exchequer, became increasingly obsessed with balancing the budget and blocked more expenditure by central and local government making further reform impossible.

The British Empire Exhibition of April 1924 was another opportunity for Labour to show itself loyal to the Crown, and counter any suggestion that it was unpatriotic. It was mounted at Wembley with many of the buildings meant to be temporary and demolished afterwards, although several were of substantial concrete construction and required a good deal of planning and building. The ostensible aims of the exhibition, which cost £12 million, was to stimulate colonial trade and strengthen the bonds of empire. There were three main buildings: the Palaces of Engineering, Industry and the

Arts as well as the Empire Pool and Empire Stadium, and a special train loop laid to connect the exhibition site to London's Marylebone Station.

There were fears that the building work would not be completed on time for the official opening on 23 April 1924, and Clynes was involved in the planning and the discussions in Cabinet. There was anxiety about building workers going on strike and delaying completion of the Empire Pool. The 7,000 workers did go on strike briefly, but Clynes was relieved when they returned to work and completed the building on time. He attended the official ceremony that opened the exhibition with much pomp and ceremony, and was pleased that 'patriotic feelings' had won the day. It certainly turned into a large propaganda exercise of celebration for the Empire with a Pageant of Empire held on 21 July 1924, for Edward composed the 'Empire March'7

The Prime Minister seemed obsessed with the need to reassure the established order that Labour was no threat to the status quo, placating the King and worrying over the Red flag being sung at Labour Party rallies. King George V liked MacDonald and got on well with him, and the latter soon felt at home in the royal company at Windsor Castle or Buckingham Palace. Anything that suggested Labour might be a threat to the established alarmed MacDonald, and placating the Establishment seemed to be more important than pursuing reform, or perhaps became a substitute for it. Despite a pledge to abolish hereditary titles in 1923, Labour created new hereditary peerages for Sydney Oliver and MacDonald's friend, C.B. Thompson. This shocked Clynes who dis-

approved of all hereditary honours, but there were more
to come. In April 1924 MacDonald awarded a baronetcy
to Alexander Grant, who owned MacVitie and Price the
biscuit manufacture. He had recently provided the use
of a Daimler car to the Prime Minister and the interest
on £40,000 to help meet some of the prime ministerial
expenses. There was much critical comment about this
in the *Daily Mail* and other papers with Labour accused
accused of selling titles, and it looked as if MacDonald
might be blundering into an early termination of the
government.

MacDonald was often away on foreign affairs at
which he was rather more successful than on the home
scene. He was a strong believer in the League of Nations
and succeeded in moderating some of the more harsh
for German reparations. The acceptance of the Dawes
Plan, by which reparation payments were reduced, was
partly due to MacDonald's policy of reconciliation which
helped ease international tensions. With MacDonald at
Locarno and elsewhere, Clynes faced problems in the
House of Commons where the government was under
the constant threat of defeat on a number of votes of
no confidence. Fortunately for him these were survived
but only because it suited the Liberals to delay a general
election, but it would be only a matter of time before the
government fell.

The Liberals were rapidly losing patience with the
government and ready to challenge it, as over the
agreement with Russia. They claimed MacDonald had
given recognition to the Russia government, as the ruler
of the former Russian Empire, without first obtaining a

guarantee of recompense for British bondholders who had lost out in the revolution. They were joined in this by the Tories, who saw recognition as strengthening the power of the Communist International. Then further complications arose over the Campbell case, in which the editor of the *Workers' Weekly* was charged with inciting troops to mutiny in an article. But the Attorney General, Patrick Hastings, withdrew the prosecution after a Cabinet discussion. The Conservatives contended this was a purely political move, and when Parliament re-assembled after the recess a vote of censure was moved in the Commons.

MacDonald was tired, and did not seem that reluctant to hold a general election, writing in his diary that he was 'inclined to give the Liberals an election….if they force it….The conditions of office perhaps bribe me to take this chance of ending the present regime.'8 After the opposition had tabled their censure motions, he appeared almost relieved when the Liberals finally voted with the Conservatives and Labour lost the vote by 364 to 198 votes. Accepting this as a vote of no confidence, MacDonald resigned and a general election was called.

Despite all the uncertainty and pressure, Clynes was less defeatist than MacDonald, and thought that the combined political opposition was the result of Labour's success rather than errors or omissions, given the constraints it was under. When the Labour government took office neither the Liberals nor the Tories thought it would succeed, but the former thought they could control it. The government's proposals for improving workers protection, working conditions of miners, more safety for women and children had all been obstructed by the opposition parties. But after eight months Labour had shown what it could do in housing, education and road building, while Clynes thought the Liberals had become afraid for their own future and started looked for an excuse to eject Labour from power, so sided with the Tories to get them out. This view passed into Labour legend to explain the defeat 1924, a conspiracy of reactionary forces determined to dig Labour out of office.9

There was considerable confidence in Labour's election campaign, with MacDonald making a series of tours around the country, speaking at large gatherings of supporters. In Birmingham he addressed a meeting of 15,000 in Birmingham and 20,000 at Huddersfield, but apart from hoping to receive credit for its eight months in power, Labour had done little to inspire the voters. The right-wing press tried to frighten its readers once again into believing that another Labour government meant communist influence and subversion. Clynes was campaigning in Manchester when the *Daily Mail* printed the so-called Zinoviev Letter, five days before polling on the 5 October 1924. The headlines screamed about a was a plot to instigate civil war by socialists on the orders of Gregori Zinoviev, president of the Communist International. In fact the letter was a forgery, written by exiled anti-Bolsheviks and planted in the Foreign Office by British intelligence with Conservative Central Office. The release was deliberately timed to cause the maximum embarrassment for Labour, and without allowing time for any investigation into its authenticity.

But after the Campbell affair, it may have carried some credibility with many undecided voters and some damage to Labour was probably done.

Clynes felt that MacDonald's reaction to the affair was timid and obstinate. With the *Daily Mail* full of lurid stories of Russian gold and Bolshevik terrorism, he just announced that he had asked the Foreign Office to find out if the letter was genuine instead of denouncing it as a forgery. Clynes saw this as just timid and obstinate, and the rest of the campaign was fought in a very bitter atmosphere. In Manchester Platting, the Tory candidate organised a considerable campaign against Clynes and there was other more sinister opposition. Once, while addressing a public meeting a procession of white clad figures entered the hall causing screaming and mayhem. There were scuffles and then open fighting between the opposing sides, and in the end the Klansman, for they claimed to be a UK branch of the Ku Klux Klan, were kicked out by some burly Labour stewards.10

The Tory campaign was much better organised, with a national network of constituency agents and a well-funded campaign, supported by an overwhelmingly right right-wing press. The Tories won 419 seats, Labour 151, while the Liberals were reduced to 42 seats. Despite this disappointment the Labour vote actually increased again to 5,551,5494 million votes or 33% of the electorate from 4,348,379. Clynes retained his seat in Manchester Platting with a majority of over a thousand, an increase since 1923. As he stood waiting for the result in the Platting Picture Theatre, which was being used as the temporary Labour headquarters, there were conflicting rumours among the large crowd. There were also thousands waiting outside on the streets and when the news of his win came through, he was carried in a chair over the heads of the crowd and for ten minutes he was unable to get a hearing.11

Herbert Parker, Clynes' nephew, had stood unsuccessfully in the safe Tory seat of Richmond in Surrey. After leaving Cambridge early, he had a series of jobs in journalism, including briefly as editor of the *Radio Times* and on the *Daily Herald*. But his experiences in the war may have continued having a psychological effect, as they did on so many veterans moving from job to job and unable to settle. He was a talented man, a convinced socialist and a Labour councillor in West Ham, but he became increasingly dependent on alcohol. Eventually his alcoholism worsened and he abandoned his family, although Clynes paid for him to have several expensive curative treatments. After his death, possibly from suicide, the Clynes family remained friendly with his widow and their two children who often spent the holidays with them at Brightlingsea.12

The 1924 election was a landslide win for the Conservatives, and gave them an overall majority of 211 seats. The disillusionment with MacDonald's leadership was soon evident, especially among the 'Red Clydesiders, and before long the issue was again being raised about Labour leaders wasting time with royal garden parties and consorting with the aristocracy, while socialism seemed farther away than ever.10 However, it was soon clear that the Baldwin government had few answers to the economic and industrial problems, a situation that was made more stark by its huge majority and a largely impotent opposition. The government benches were often half-empty with many of its MPs absent from parliamentary business, no doubt feeling secure in the knowledge that the government was in no danger.

In 1925 Clynes went off himself for three weeks to Denmark as a guest of a bacon manufacturer who he had got to know during his time as Minister for Food. He was impressed by the co-operative farming methods he saw, the high wages and living standards, with family farms organised into co-operatives run on a profit-share basis. But at home there were mounting problems in the coal-mining industry and rising unemployment. Since the end of the war there had been steady deflation with a fall in prices and wages. In April 1925 there was a return to the Gold Standard and to pre-war parity with the US dollar in an effort to restore London's pre-war position in the international money markets. But the effect was to damage exports, push down wages, while the National Debt grew alarmingly and the pound grew became overvalued in relation to the dollar.

The coal mining industry was heavily hit as it had been largely unmodernised with little capital investment and unable to compete with foreign mines. As it was labour intensive with high wage costs, the mine owners decided to end the existing wage agreements and requested lower wages for longer hours of work. The miner's union protested loudly and threatened to strike. Clynes first speech in the House on returning from Denmark was on the sufferings of the miners, but he saw that Tory benches remained implacable in their response with their 'slightly contemptuous faces round us never changed; or if they did it was merely to express by a fleeting glance a well-bred deprecation of our ungentlemanly violence.'13

The Baldwin government appointed a commission to look into the coal mining problems, and in the meanwhile the employers were be paid a subsidy to maintain the miners wages. When the Samuel Commission reported in March 1926 it recommended lower wages and increased hours, precisely what the owners had wanted. The leaders of the miners union, A.J. Cook and Herbert Smith, refused to discuss wage reductions while the Mining Association, representing employers, only offered a wage reduction of 13 per cent and a return to an eight hour day. A nationwide coal miners strike was called, and it was soon clear that the other unions were sympathetic and supportive, but at this stage few thought it would lead to a general stoppage. But without widespread support it was unlikely that the miner's strike would have much effect, particularly as the government was prepared to use its full emergency powers.

The King was extremely alarmed and, although expressing sympathy for the miners, thought a widespread strike could be the beginning of a revolution, and 'supposed all this (with a gesture indicating his surroundings) will vanish.'15 However, moderate trade union leaders were less than enthusiastic about a general stoppage Several, such as Ernest Bevin and Margaret Bondfield, were not present when the TUC approved of a general strike. They were very angry, but it was too late and the strike began on 4 May 1926. Some of the coal surface workers, who were members of the GMWU, were involved and about half of them eventually came out on strike in sympathy. Throughout the strike the GMWU National Executive kept in close touch with the strikers, and set up an emergency committee, that included both Clynes and Thorne, to liaise on a daily basis.

The strike was initially solid, and there was an optimism throughout the labour movement that victory would soon be achieved. There was little violence and vehicles carrying essential supplies were allowed through by the pickets, but it gradually became clear the dispute would be drawn out. The government emergency measures proved increasingly efficient with volunteers unloading and moving food supplies from the docks, as well as driving buses and trams. Although the press was muzzled by the striking printers, the government put out the *British Gazette* run by Churchill, and full of anti-strike propaganda. The BBC radio service came under pressure to put over the government point of view in news bulletins, and when it did succumb was probably in breach of its charter.

The government was threatening to call out more troops and the TUC to call out more unions on strike when the Liberal Sir John Simon, who opposed the strike anyway, declared it to be illegal and the men involved liable to be sued for damages. On the eighth day of the strike Herbert Samuel offered to mediate on the basis of his report and the TUC, which was glad of the opportunity, accepted his offer and called off the strike on 12 May. The Prime Minister asked employers employers to take back their striking workers, but there were many reprisals and harsher condition for re-employment, with the railwaymen having to promise never to go on such a strike again. Within a few days almost all resistance had ended, and the miners were on their own to carry on with their strike. They did so until December 1926 when even they had to give in amid considerable anger and bitterness at their 'betrayal' by government, the trade unions, and the Labour Party. Their wages were cut and hours increased with future negotiations put on a regional basis.

The GMWU supported the TUC decision to call off the strike, with strong reservations about its wisdom from the beginning. Clynes was most vociferous in his opposition:

> a strike would be a national disaster, and a fatal step to Union prestige....A national strike if complete, would inflict starvation first and most on the poorest of the population. Riot or disorder could not feed them, and nay appeal to force would inevitably be answered by superior force. How could such an action benefit the working classes?14

Clynes, like so many of his trade union colleagues, shrunk from the threat to the established order which the General Strike represented. He was very busy during the strike with the affairs of his own union, which had to pay its own members on strike and help other unions with loans and grants. The financial impact on the coffers of the GMWU was serious, 82,000 members had received strike pay by the 4th of May. However, by the end of August all but 8,000, almost all colliery surface workers, had returned to work. Even this had cost the union £6,000 a week and they had to keep up payments until the end by which time their funds were rapidly depleting. The union paid out £240,000 in total strike pay by the end, equivalent to over £13 million in monetary value to-day, and it had weakened the union enormously. Any further expansion plans involving capital expenditure had to be postponed including the construction of a new headquarters building in central London, something the TGWU achieved in 1928 with the opening of Transport House. Part of this building was leased to the Labour Party as its headquarters, no doubt to Ernest Bevin's satisfaction, making the union the party's landlord.15

Although opposed to the strike, Clynes was torn by his sympathy for the miners but convinced that direct action was bound to fail. He believed the strike weapon should only be used as the last resort in a trade dispute, not as a political weapon to fight the cause of the working class in general. This should always be done through the ballot box and the Labour Party, as the political arm of labour movement. But the dilemma was that without a Labour government in power how could the working class expect truth, justice and honesty to prevail, and with the government safeguarding the interests of capital? The ignorance and class prejudice expressed from the Tory benches and from some Liberals during the strike shocked Clynes, so he appreciated the frustration and anger of those who felt that Labour should have have given more support to the strike.

Despite the disillusion of many with the Labour Party Clynes persisted in believing that the lesson of the strike was that the only way to reform was through the ballot box, and not by extra-parliamentary resistance.16 There had actually been little violence during the strike, while the government had shown itself only too willing to use state violence if thought necessary against the strikers. The prospect of the strike escalating into some form of violent revolution was a scare mongering myth used by by the right-wing press, which suited some sections of the government. The link between the strike and some kind of communist plot to overthrow the state was a propaganda tool more than anything relating to the truth, although no doubt it was a genuine fear in the minds of many.

Although he was constantly criticised for a lack of class solidarity in the strike when the unions, notably the miners and railwaymen, were fighting for their life, Clynes continued to argue the case for the futility of a total stoppage. He believed that the main victims of such actions were always likely to be the strikers and their families, especially in longer disputes. He made this this clear to the GMWU Congress in 1926:

> Manifestations of solidarity are admirable, but solidarity without wisdom worthless, and the heroics of the first few days fighting fade into the sacred and subdued murmurs of defeated and distracted men.16

In the years that followed the Labour Party was put on the defensive by warnings in the right wing press about the dangers of communist subversion. The 1917 Russian Revolution was seen by some on the left as an attempt to build a socialist society, an example of what could be achieved by socialist planning. But Labour was clearly committed to a constitutional path towards socialism, which meant carrying the people with it to the ballot box. But it had to battle against constant propaganda seeking to make democratic socialism seem synonymous with Soviet communism.

To add to the difficulties were the activities of the British Communist Party, which was attracting many new members among the working class in industrial, areas, especially in mining seats across central Scotland and South Wales, and it was soon a real threat and rival to Labour in those areas. The CPGB made the constant demand for 'working class unity,' and frequent appeals for the Labour Party to join in this process. This goes some way to explain the lack of support among Labour MPs in the 1926 strike, for fear of being associated with Communist subversion.

In the early days of the Communist Party many ILP members and trade union activists were sympathetic, including Clynes. They were even willing to accept Communist members into the Labour Party until the strong allegiance of the CPGB to the USSR after 1917 became apparent. Thereafter Communist Party members were banned from being card carrying members of the Labour Party, and the communists became increasingly anti-Labour. Their antagonism to Labour seemed to be at times greater than their opposition to capitalism itself, and many Labour leaders were the object of personal abuse and even libellous attacks, including Clynes. The CPGB did all it could to damage the reputations of the trade union and Labour leaders, accusing them of betraying the working class and worse, while the outcome of the General Strike gave them plenty of ammunition.

Like all trade unions, the GMWU was faced with the problem of Communist infiltration. In the immediate post-war years the union had not been antagonistic towards the Communist Party and its members, but the party's decision to form the National Minority Movement in 1924 marked a change in relations. The aim of the NMM was to organise a radical presence in the trade union movement by cultivating those workers who were dissatisfied with the existing leadership. It became influential very rapidly in some unions, particularly the coal miners whose secretary, A.J. Cook, was an NMM member. It was also influential in urging a general strike and in spreading pro-strike propaganda, again notably in the coal fields. All this alarmed the moderate union leaders like Clynes, who were always in a majority on the TUC General Council. In 1925 the GMWU executive decided to take unilateral action against the NMM, and consulted all district secretaries on the activities of front organisations. As a result the GMWU decided to break off all contacts with the Communist Party, disaffiliate from all Trade Councils that recognised the NMM, and to cease giving financial help to Communist Party candidates in local elections.17

But the Communists already had a strong presence in many GMWU branches, mainly in Scotland, from where the national leadership faced considerable criticism of their anti-Communist measures. The Glasgow No 23 Branch, for example, protested the veto and several branches continued to support the NMM on Glasgow Trades Council. The GMWU National Executive was adamant that its authority should not be flouted in this way by local branches, but the revolt nevertheless spread to some London branches in February 1927, and some members sought to attend the NMM annual conference which had been forbidden. The GMWU Executive reiterated that members of the union could not also join the CPGB and the NMM, neither could CPGB be union officials or hold any post in the union, and all those officials attending the NMM conference were suspended.

The Communists continued with their infiltration efforts, however, and regularly put up candidates for election to union positions. Clynes, Thorne and the GMWU Executive were so concerned that they were prepared to bolster their position with an amendment to the union rulebook which stated that officers, including the General Secretary and President, would be granted permanent tenure rather than having to stand for regular re-election. This desperate measure was carried at the 1926 Biennial Conference of the union accompanied by a good deal of pressure from the Executive. But it was controversial and sparked considerable protest, attacked as grossly undemocratic by the Communists and some others on the left.18

Clynes thought the dictatorship of the proletariat was inherently undemocratic and likely to lead to regime that was totalitarian, as was becoming increasingly clear in the Soviet Union. The need to counter Communist, as well as right-wing propaganda was more than just an irritant to Labour but took up a great deal of time and energy. The communists were particularly relentless in their pro-ganda through the *Daily Worker*, party pamphlets and its front organizations. In this respect Clynes felt were the CPGB was more help Labour's parliamentary and other enemies, who were able to lump all groups on the left together, ignoring their intense rivalry.

The police raid on the Soviet Arcos trade organisation in London, and the Zinoviev letter, showed how highly dangerous this could be, especially when candidates who stood against Labour in elections syphoned off votes by using 'Red Scare' tactics. The Communists usually lost their deposits, and in the 1924 election only one CPGB MP was elected, while the Communist candidate who opposing Clynes in Manchester Platting only gained 400 votes and lost his deposit. In the 1920's, Clynes was a particular target of the Communist Party because of his willingness to serve in the wartime coalition government, for opposing the Labour exit from it in 1918, and for his attitude to the 1926 General Strike. They even invented falsehoods, such as accusing him of taking a letter from Lloyd George to the one-day conference that Labour Party held in 1918, pleading for it to stay in the coalition. which was completely untrue.19

The Baldwin government seemed adrift in a torpor on

the rising unemployment, apparently hanging on until
the election. Clynes realised that just paying out the dole
to the unemployed, at a time when the national deficit
was rising while doing nothing to tackle the problem
of unemployment, was futile.

> The Conservatives seem to think that their duty is to
> divert national money by the millions to unemployment pay,
> and that there is nothing else to do; they do not try to
> get rid of unemployment or find work for the workless; so
> long as they can proffer some kind of charity, they feel that
> their job is done.[20]

He had become convinced from his experience in the
war, that state intervention through central government
agencies could create conditions of full employment,
especially if it controlled the commanding heights of the
economy through nationalization. But even without that
this, the state could still intervene to influence the
allocation of resources and controls to create jobs. But
public ownership had to be implemented with the power
of parliamentary approval which means that Labour had
to have a clear majority, unencumbered by an economic
depression. The unemployment rate was 12% in 1926
and continued to rise in 1927 and 1928 with the government's seeming lack of urgency adding to the anger of
many people.

8
Hope and Disaster

When the general election was called in May 1929 Clynes as the Deputy Leader of the Labour Party was soon busy preparing for the campaign. The extension of the vote to women over twenty-one in 1928 meant there a larger electorate, and many of these new voters were suspected by the Tories of being sympathetic to Labour. The *Daily Mail* had argued that Labour supported the female vote vote in order to manipulate impressionable young women to vote for it! But there was no evidence for this, or even certainty about how the new female votes would go.

Once the campaign got underway the Tories and their press allies tried to revive all the old 'Red Scare' tactics, and there were posters everywhere with Baldwin's image and the slogan 'Safety First.' The message was that the people would be safer with the Conservatives, and that Labour would rock the boat. This was a perennial Tory tactic, trying to stir up fear by warnings of what Labour would have in store for voters.

It was the first election to include radio broadcasts by the party leaders, and Baldwin proved somewhat more effective in front of the microphone, sounding avuncular and reassuring. In contrast, MacDonald had difficulty in adapting his booming voice, so effective in mass public meetings, to the intimacy of the BBC studio and people's living rooms. The Labour Party manifesto made clear its socialist policies, to replace capitalism with a fairer and equable economic and social system. They included the nationalising of the Bank of England and bringing basic industries under public ownership. These aims were all described in general terms, and there was no clear time table set out for achieving them, nor any real indication indication of how they would be implemented. To some some it seemed to imply that merely stating socialist aims was sufficient, without alarming either the markets or the voters excessively. Clynes was sceptical whether the voters were ready for radical socialist reforms, and his view 'that we shall get socialism in Britain just as soon as the majority of the people in Britain want it, and that our job for the present is to go on making Socialists.'[1]

The result still gave Labour had an overall majority of seats, with 8.5 million votes and 288 MPs. The Tories were reduced to 260, and the Liberals to 53 seats, once again holding the balance of power. Clynes was surprised by even by this modest victory, and displeased once again with being in a minority government and all the constraints this imposed. But the party had still gained 137 MP's who came from a wider variety of backgrounds than previous intakes, many from the big cities and often with no trade union connections. The Liberals also did in well in votes, probably due to the effective campaigning of the party on the unemployment issue. Lloyd George's arguments seemed more cogent to many voters more than the solutions Labour had to offer. But dependence on the support of the Liberals once again made Clynes feel as if the party was like a long distance runner who finds he has a heavy weight tied to his leg.[2]

This time when MacDonald appointed his cabinet, Clynes was made Home Secretary, and his trade union colleague, Margaret Bondfield, became the first woman in the cabinet as Minister of Labour. The process of inducting the new ministers had not changed since 1922, and once again Labour's leaders presented themselves at Windsor in full morning dress to receive their seals of office from the King. Clynes was happier this time to be appointed to one of the three most senior Cabinet jobs, and relieved at not having to live in Downing Street again with all the expense and aggravation that it had brought last time.

He had hardly got his bearings in the job before he had to deal with an application for residency from Leon Trotsky, the Russian revolutionary leader. He had been living in Turkey, and had already had applications to settle in Germany turned down. In April 1929 he was visited by Sydney and Beatrice Webb, who told him they were confident that Labour was going to win the election and encouraged him to the apply for a British visa. After the election Sydney Webb became a minister, and Trotsky duly made an application to the British Consul in Constantinople for a visa. He wrote Beatrice Webb, and told her he was looking forward to working in the British Museum, and made contact with George Lansbury who had also visited. He no doubt felt that these high-level connections in the Labour Party would mean few problems in getting a visa, but he was to be disappointed.3

Many leading figures of the day campaigned for Trotsky to remain, including John Maynard Keynes, C.P.

Scott, Bernard Shaw, Arnold Bennett and the Bishop of Birmingham. But despite this, the decision was made not to grant the visa. Clynes had to inform the Cabinet that 'the admission of Trotsky to this country might be regarded as an unfriendly act by the Soviet Union, and they might allege that the British Government had given hospitality to Trotsky for political reasons and used using him as a means of weakening the existence of the government of Russia.'[4]

When Clynes informed the House of Commons of the decision he said that despite assurances about Trotsky's political activities while in the country, the government did not believe them. Even if he spent his time writing and doing research, others with less benign intention might exploit his presence. He also told the House that there was in fact no 'right' to asylum as such, and denied that the decision had anything to do with the attitude of the Soviet Union. But he was quite frank that the decision was influenced by the desire to restore more friendly relations with Russia, but left unsaid the fear that Trotsky and his followers might use the country as a base for pursuing plans to overthrow the Stalin regime. A cartoon appeared in *Punch* showing Clynes turning Trotsky away from the door despite his claim to be 'a friend of the house.' Although the decision was popular with the Conservatives and the right-wing press, it was not well received at all on the liberal left and Clynes was bitterly criticised for what was seen as a cravenly submissive attitude, and denial of the British tradition of offering sanctuary to political exiles.

When he accepted the post of Home Secretary Clynes knew that that it could rapidly undo political reputations, but he did not realise how many sleepless nights it would give him. There were masses of documents to read covering a wide range of issues, many of which were of intense interest to the press and public. These included the metropolitan police, security, and the penal system. At a time when capital punishment was still quite common, the Home Secretary had the unenviable task of making the final decision about whether death sentences should carried out.

This caused the humane and compassionate Clynes considerable anxiety, especially as he was the first Home Secretary to oppose capital punishment. He hoped that a parliamentary enquiry that had been set up would recommend abolition, but in the meantime hearing appeals for a reprieve once a death sentence had been passed after conviction in a murder trial was particularly harrowing. Unfortunately there were several notorious murder trials in 1929 and 1930 which all ended in guilty verdicts, and came to the Home Secretary on a clemency appeal. Perhaps the most notorious was the Podmore case. In January 1929 the body of a man named Vivian Messiter, an oil company agent, was discovered in a locked garage in Southampton. He had been missing for nine weeks but the celebrated pathologist, Bernard Spilsbury, was confident that death had been caused by several blows to the skull with a blunt instrument. The garage also revealed blood splatter showing it was the likely crime scene, and a receipt found that incriminated

William Podmore who had recently worked as Messiter's assistant. It showed that he had been claiming commission on sales that had not taken place. The police concluded there had been a confrontation over this, and Podmore had murdered his employer with a hammer. But the hammer was never found, and the receipt book was the most crucial piece of evidence. Podmore was found guilty and sentenced to death.5

There was a public outcry about the verdict which many felt was unsafe as the evidence against Podmore was entirely circumstantial, and this led to further protests and unease about the death sentence being carried out. When the final plea for clemency reached the Home Office, Clynes 'searched for many days in the hope that we'd find some reason for recommending a reprieve. I searched in vain.' The evidence, although circumstantial, was strong and Podmore was probably guilty, but there was an area of doubt that might have made a capital sentence inappropriate. But Clynes was advised there were no grounds for revoking the death sentence under the law as it then was, so he rejected the appeal.5

When sitting at home in Putney one evening reading, Clynes heard a knock on the front door. On opening it he found a figure standing dimly in the shadows a few yards away. The man said in a quiet voice that he had come to speak about the hammer in the Podmore case. Clynes replied that it would be improper for him to discuss such a matter privately and he would see the man at the Home Office the next morning. The next day he gave instructions for the person to be brought to him, but he never appeared and the mysterious visitor was never seen again.6 In this case, as with all the other death sentence appeals with which he dealt, there there were thousands of letters from the public pleading clemency, many from women promising to keep the murderer on the straight and narrow if reprieved.

The parliamentary committee reviewing capital punishment was continuing its work, and there was a lively public debate on the issue, with newspapers taking sides for and against. Clynes felt able to grant several reprieves in 1930, and only four executions took place that year. When the committee did report, it recommended that capital punishment should be suspended for five years so that the effects could be ascertained. But the Tories refused to cooperate, and new legislation was not forthcoming.

It seems amazing today, when government ministers are so well protected, that anyone could have so easily discovered the private address of the Home Secretary and called on him without any problem. As soon as he was appointed, Clynes was approached by a burly man in plain clothes who explained that he was from Special Branch and that he, a car, and a chauffeur were at his disposal. At first Clynes declined the offer thinking this special protection was unnecessary but his experiences made him change his mind.7

One afternoon a woman called unannounced at the Clyne's home, and when shown into the drawing room declared that she was spending the weekend with them.

The problem was always how to usher such visitors out of the house, without causing offence or attracting too much attention. On another occasion a man called and began speaking quite lucidly about government policy, and made suggestions that Clynes politely acknowledged as sensible. They then shook hands and the man left without incident, but a few days later Clynes learned he had blown his brains out in his room at a London hotel. Another caller who appeared to be quite sane said she had come to warn him about certain London gang members who were out to cause him harm. She assured him that these gangs were always able to evade detection, and gave Clynes graphic descriptions of the kind of injuries they could inflict. She got quite hysterical about these dangers, but was led out and went quietly away.8

Some police presence was clearly in order and a policeman was stationed outside his home at all times, but this did not stop the invasion of privacy. One morning Mary Clynes and her daughter were having breakfast in the front room of their house when there was the sudden noise of smashing glass. When Clynes rushed down the stairs, he entered the room and saw a woman looking in through the hole in a window she had just smashed with a chopper in each hand. Mary Clynes and daughter were standing terrified between the table and the door. The policeman had just moved off a few yards on his beat and had missed the woman entering the garden gate, crossing the small lawn and smashing every front ground floor window.9

When the policeman did arrive and interrogate the woman it appeared she had a long-running dispute over litigation, and as the Home Secretary was in charge of the courts she somehow held him responsible for her problems. It turned out later that she was a well-educated middle-class lady who had travelled from her home in York to Putney, purchased the choppers in a local ironmongers shop and brought them wrapped in newspaper to Clynes address. When the maid told her that she could only see the Home Secretary at his office, she went along the front lawn smashing all the windows. To add insult to injury Clynes had to pay to have all the windows replaced at a cost of £14, as there were no government funds available to cover such a contingency. The lady was subsequently dealt with by a local magistrate whose windows she threatened also to smash unless she got redress![10]

Despite these alarms, Clyne found he was able to do some good as Home Secretary in the areas of working conditions, health and safety. He made visits to many works and factories, even climbing high buildings and scaffolding to see for himself the dangers faced by construction workers on a daily basis. The enormous new power station was being built at Battersea, and there had already been several deaths and serious accidents, mainly caused by falls from the wooden scaffolding and from high cranes overturning. He went to the site, and climbed the seven or eight stories of platforms beside the huge chimneys, and had a panoramic view of the machinery below and dangers that cost workers lives.

But he found it impossible to avoid some of the ceremonial duties that he disliked. Some led to bizarre situations, none more so than the birth of Princess Margaret Rose to the Duke and Duchess of Kent. He was informed it was traditonal for the Home Secretary to attend royal births to ensure there was no dangers of substitution, or other identity problems with an heir to the throne. Clynes travelled up to Glamis Castle where he stayed as a guest of Lady Airlie.

There were huge crowds everywhere, and he received a warm welcome. Soon he was told his attendance was required at the castle, so he waited in a downstairs room. After a while he was asked to go to an anti-room where he found a gathering of the King, a doctor, nurses and a few others waiting around. The baby, who might have one day become the monarch, was brought in to be shown to everyone. After leaving, Clynes had to fill out a certificate of birth for the child and send telegrams to various dignatories such as the Lord Mayor of London who would then send word for the bells of St. Paul's to be rung.11

In October 1929 the collapse of prices on the New York Stock Exchange marked the start of a world-wide economic depression. With the fall in commodity prices and the spread of unemployment in the United States, other countries began to feel the effects. The cycle of debt, by which US money was paid to Germany to pay its war reparations to Britain, was adversely affected. Foreign investors withdrew funds from the London money market, gold began to move out of Britain and the value of the pound started to slide. It affected all the

1. J.H. Thomas, MacDonald, Clynes and Henderon arrive to meet the King after the 1923 election

2. Clynes and Mary in the 1920's

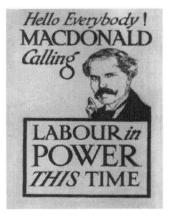

3. Labour election poster 1929

THE LABOUR CABINET, 1929.

4. Labour Cabinet 1929

5. MacDonald with Baldwin 1931   6. The Clynes in retirement

the basic industries, and unemployment began to rise. The Chancellor of the Exchequer, Philip Snowden, continued to trust in orthodox financial policies, and cutting public expenditure to try to rescue the national debt. In his budget of 1930 income tax was raised to 4s 6d in the pound, and surtax was increased. He sought to balance the budget as if the national economy were some kind of giant household, seen as essential to maintain national and international confidence in Britain. This was the 'Treasury view' and Snowden, 'small and dogged,' stuck to it in the face of mounting evidence that it would not work.

Despite some reservations, all the Cabinet gave their support to Snowden and Clynes felt that 'no man could have done more' even though unemployment did not stop rising. The strange situation was that although Clynes despaired at the rise of unemployment, he did not see any connection between deflationary economic policy and rising unemployment despite realising that the state were able to create jobs. The view was that public expenditure would weaken the pound and lead to devaluation which he seemed to have accepted as more important than managing unemployment. There were a few targeted measures put in place, including some new road building, railway improvements as well as the raising of the school leaving age to fifteen. But these had little effect on unemployment which was rising faster than new jobs could be created by these tentative measures.

In November 1929 an Unemployment Insurance Bill extended unemployment benefit payments, but the crisis was making divisions in the Labour movement worse.

The ILP led by James Maxton, was increasingly critical of the lack of radical solutions to unemployment, and the ILP was by now behaving as a separate party which led to MacDonald, a member since 1898, to resign his membership. The decisions on economic policy were taken by a small group of Cabinet ministers consisting of MacDonald, Snowden, and Henderson. Clynes was excluded, possibly because he was so close to the trade unions and might have demanded more action to deal with unemployment, even though he remained publicly supportive of the orthodox line.

MacDonald abhorred class conflict of any kind, and took every opportunity to steer the Labour Party away from it. He was largely ignorant of modern economic thinking and indifferent to the socialist feelings among the wider party membership, with now an almost total complete disdain for the ILP. Snowden also mistrusted the trade unions, and shared a similar contempt for the ILP, even though he also had risen within it. He was convinced that social justice was compatible with fiscal rectitude, and when they did come into conflict, the latter would have to prevail.12

There was an effort to dangle the possibility of electoral reform in front of the Liberals, hoping they might then approve more radical solutions to the unemployment problem, but a proposed electoral reform bill got stuck in the second chamber. More Labour MPs were growing rebellious, including Oswald Mosley, the young renegade ex-Tory now in the cabinet. He presented a memorandum of proposals for reducing unemployment. It suggested a massive programme of job creating in a virtually command economy with road building and other infra-structure projects, new tariffs, and the creation a state finance corporation to invest in restructuring industry. This was totally opposed by the Treasury and almost all the Cabinet. Clynes considered it 'quite fantastic,' and saw some of proposals in the Mosley Memorandum as 'approaching insanity.'13

The General and Municipal Workers Union had at first been highly supportive of the Labour government. It had in Clynes and Bondfield, two senior officials in the Cabinet in addition to eighteen members who were MPs, six of whom were sponsored by the union. So it therefore had considerable hope that the interests of its members and the wider labour movement would be promoted and safeguarded. However,the executive were soon disappointed when there was little sign of any economic recovery, with much of industry cutting wages in response falling demand. The trade unions, therefore, became increasingly disillusioned and desperate.

In several disputes the union was thrown on to the defensive in futile negotiations with employers knowing it was in a weak negotiating position. The meetings of the GMWU Executive and General Council were more pessimistic and bitter about the situation, which placed Clynes and Bondfield in a difficult situation. Although Will Thorne was supportive, he was an ordinary back-bencher and not in the Government, but he too was concerned with the union's falling membership and its industry weakness.14

In the Budget of 1930, Snowden showed that he was still in the grip of the same financial orthodoxy, unable or unwilling to think outside the orthodox, and supported in a rather sheep-like way by the rest of the Cabinet including Clynes. Despite knowing the dire situation of his union members, Clynes still thought there was no alternative, and sang the praises of the Chancellor, asserting of Snowden that 'no man could have done more.' Within his limitations this might have seem true, but there was much more he could have done if he had been able to grasp alternative possibilities. But his fiscal rectitude, hostility to the trade unions and the ILP meant he was always likely to stick to an orthodox course. By July 1931 unemployment figures had reached 2,750,000 and seemed out of control, and a committee set up to investigate and make recommendations.

It consisted entirely of businessmen, and was likely to report in a way favourable to the interests of finance and business. The mystery is why it was set up, given that its recommendations were so predictable, and likely to lead to a crisis of decision-making by the Cabinet. When the May Committee's Report was published it forecast a public deficit of £120 million, and recommended pay cuts for teachers, civil servants and other public sector employees, in addition to a 20% reduction in unemployment benefit. On the same day, July 31 1931, as the May Committee reported, Snowden issued a warning in House of Commons about the size of the budget deficit, unless considerable economies were imposed with all due haste.

Every week the unemployment figures continued to rise with the Tories making the absurd claim that economic conditions were all the fault of Labour rather than world conditions, and that their profligate spending was driving the country towards bankruptcy. The Liberals, who had also lost their earlier beliefs in fighting the slump with an expansionary budget, now feared the consequences of an increased public expenditure more, adding their weight to the pressure for economies. On 11 August the King sent his private secretary to see MacDonald to talk about the the crisis, but the Prime Minister was reticent about what was discussed which some raised suspicions in Cabinet.

If the projected deficit of £120 million was reached, cuts of £78 million in spending were needed to avoid a devaluation with unemployment benefit cuts seeming to be inevitable. These draconian measures met with some some opposition in the Cabinet, including Clynes, but a majority were still supportive of cuts. On 21 August a TUC delegation met with MacDonald and his closest cabinet colleagues, making it clear that unemployment benefit cuts were unacceptable to the trade unions, and suggesting a reduction in public sector salaries instead. When the Cabinet voted, it was twelve to nine in favour of cuts, with the opposition now including both Clynes and Henderson. Although still supporting the austerity measures in general, they were just as worried about the splits opening up in the Labour movement.

MacDonald and Snowden reassured the Cabinet that an election would not be called, or any new party formed even if the cuts were not approved. But MacDonald still refused the attend the Commons to meet concerned Labour MPs, or to propose any plans for the delay of the crisis. On the 31 August, MacDonald went to see the King, and this visit was followed immediately by that of Baldwin and Herbert Samuel. This added to the drama of the situation, and Clynes thought it only made the situation worse. He was made uneasy by the the coming and goings, secret discussions, meetings and consultations that that were now taking place with many parties, while nobody in the cabinet or the party seemed to have any clear idea about what was going on.

The cabinet plodded on every day, discussing the various proposals for dealing with the crisis, and for a time MacDonald seemed to agree with some of the alternatives considered, although his mind often seemed to be elsewhere, and was constantly distracted. It was then decided to raise interest rates, with further borrowing to support the pound. By now, Clynes, and most of the Cabinet were determined to resist any further plans to reduce wages or unemployment benefit, even though they accepted them as an ultimate option. In the mean MacDonald continued reassuring them that there would be no change of government or a general election.12

At this stage, MacDonald seemed to suddenly change his mind, and disagreement in the Cabinet was allowed to come into the open. It was clear to Clynes that there were now two options: abandon the unemployed as the prime minister seemed ready to do, or to resign from the government. It had come to a point at which all his emotional commitment to he labour movement over-rode any residual loyalty remaining towards MacDonald or the government, and he was now 'preferred to lose anything personally rather than my self-respect and my happiness.' As the Cabinet broke up and the members exited from 10 Downing Street into the dimly lit street, Clynes saw the unforgettable impression of their faces ranging from astonishment, despair, and on a few even avarice and triumph.13

MacDonald then resigned, but instead of going into opposition was invited by the King to form a temporary National Government. This was largely on the advice of Herbert Samuel, but it flattered MacDonald and appealed to his vanity. His agreeing to form a coalition government was a tremendous shock to his Cabinet colleagues, particularly in view of his recent reassurances. He still hoped to carry his Labour colleagues into the coalition, but completely mismanaged the situation, presenting them with a *fait accompli* instead of trying to persuade them. Despite attempts to bribe individuals, such as the offer of a peerage for Henderson, only four ministers, including Snowden and Thomas, and fourteen Labour MPs followed him into the new government. Clynes went with the other ministers to hand in their seals of office at Buckingham Palace in an atmosphere 'solemn and funereal' as ministers entered one by one and placed the red boxes containing their seals on to a table next to George V, bowed and took their leave.14

Two days after the government's resignation Clynes, Margaret Bondfield and the other sponsored MPs were called before the GMWU National Executive to explain their behaviour. Clynes claimed to have been wholly consistent as he had always supported cuts in wasteful expenditure such as armaments, but had opposed reductions in unemployment pay that would have had a direct impact on working men and their families. He had 'resolutely refused to give support to any reduction in unemployment pay.....if the alternative was to resign he decided upon resignation rather than submission.'15 Bondfield who, as Minister of Labour, was more directly responsible for unemployment benefit and supported supported the cuts to the end, was questioned more critically and her political reputation never recovered. The executive then endorsed the decision of the two ex-ministers to refuse to serve in the new administration.

MacDonald was expelled from the Labour Party, and Clynes was asked to take over as the temporary leader. Writing in his diary, Hugh Dalton recorded that 'Clynes says that 'Uncle' (Henderson) has strongly urged him to be the leader but he realises that in view of all that has happened, that 'Uncle' is surely the only possible choice .....For himself, he has been so long in the Movement, that he no longer has any undue ambitions. But he has still not lost the love of service.'16 But he also felt that Henderson deserved the post more, and urged him to accept.

A few days MacDonald, once again Prime Minister, named his new Cabinet and all three who had left Labour with him were in it. Clynes now sadly reflected that although MacDonald had contributed greatly to the early Labour Party, he owed it far more than he gave.

His whole life had been spent trying to convince people about the benefits of socialism, and he should have dealt with the crisis by applying those principles. Like most of his colleagues, Clynes had not thought MacDonald was capable of acting as he did, and betraying the party by stepping aside from his own people to lead the opposition forces. He later claimed it was only at the that everything became clear, when they had handed in their resignations and MacDonald had returned from the palace. He hardly concealed his satisfaction in telling them that everything was now changed, except for himself who was to remain as the Prime Minister. It was then evident that he had planned the whole scenario, and made promises he had no intention of keeping. All had been broken, not least that the new government was to be temporary and not a permanent coalition. As a young man, and even into middle-age, MacDonald had been vigorous and quite courageous but with age his courage declined, and he became increasingly obscure, always looking for the safe option and never willing to take risks based on honestly held principles. 17

From August to November 1931 the new government only had ten cabinet ministers, four former Labour ministers, four Conservatives including, Stanley Baldwin and Neville Chamberlain, and two Liberals. MacDonald could now be open about his disdain for the Party that now regarded him as a traitor. The arguments for and against MacDonald, and the decisions he took, have been widely discussed in great detail ever since. He is still seen by many as the man who betrayed the Labour Party for the sake of his own ambition and vanity, and there is evidence both for and against. But criticisms of of him must take account of the context, and castigating MacDonald should not ignore the fact that in 1931 he did have to act in the national interest, not just in that of the Labour Party, and it has been argued that in doing so he paved the way for an eventual economic recovery. He and Snowden could hardly have applied the new demand management theories of Keynes which in a less than fully formed state. And reflating the economy would have meant more state control than the established order would have tolerated, including the Liberal Party, on whose votes the government was still dependent.18

When parliament re-assembled on 8 September 1931 Labour MPs faced the serried ranks of the new National Coalition government. As Clynes sat on the opposition Front Bench he could see the faces of men who had been his colleagues for a quarter of a century. The government turned immediately to financial problems, and Snowden's proposed an emergency Budget increasing income tax and cutting public sector wages of public by 10%. In the ensuing debate both the Tories and the Liberals supported the Budget, but only twelve Labour MPs did so. Even so, the government had a surprisingly small majority of fifty, although Labour was in a difficult situation, making it clear it opposed any cuts in unemployment benefit without offering any alternative to the governments policies. MacDonald sat silently in his place only too aware of the hostility towards him and the dislike which was almost palpable across the floor. To Clynes he seemed almost bowed down by it, but the budget cuts had an almost immediate effect with the USA giving credits worth £80 million which stopped the decline in the value of the pound. But funds continued to be withdrawn, and it looked as if the country's credit would be soon exhausted. The government responded by suspending the gold standard, and the value of the pound fell by a quarter on the foreign exchanges.

Labour was in disarray, with few people able or willing to make a convincing case for a socialist solution to the economic crisis, and all they could do was oppose the cuts without offering an alternative. When a general election was called, the government was able to claim that the measures taken by the coalition had saved the economy from complete collapse. At the Labour Party conference in Scarborough, progressive proposals were debated, as the party tried to pull itself together and agree a programme for the coming election. But the chances of Labour being defeated were high, especially with the 'first past the post' voting system.

One of the casualties of the Labour government's fall was the electoral reform bill that Clynes had finally proposed in August 1931, as the Representation of the People's Bill, and which was the culmination of two years discussion and manoeuvre with the Liberals. It was clear to both the Liberals and Labour that they suffered from the unfair distribution of votes to seats under the current electoral system, and both had some interest in reform. But MacDonald was implacably opposed to a proportional representation system, so the alternative vote system offered some compromise. A proposal had been included in the King's Speech in 1929, and that led to a Speakers Conference considering reform. However, that too was a casualty of the political crisis and the ensuing change of government. So the 1931 election and subsequent ones were fought on the simple majority voting system that was likely to continue benefiting the Tories.

9

In The Wilderness

For MacDonald it seemed a promising moment to seek public endorsement of the new government, and an election was called for 14 October 1931. Although demoralised and confused, the Labour Party was at at least determined to fight a vigorous campaign. When Clynes travelled north to Manchester he found much public uneasiness and worry about the economy. The voters seemed to want clarity and reassurance, and the mood of fear got worse as the campaign proceeded. There was a bitter and unpleasant atmosphere of propaganda, half-truths, and lies mainly coming from the coalition government and its press allies.

However, Labour could not avoid the election being fought largely on its record in office, and inability to find solutions to the economic problems. The Prime Minister, and his ex-Labour colleagues who had joined the coalition, remarkably escaped all censure. The blame was placed squarely on those who had stayed loyal to Labour, while MacDonald soon learned the value of having the press on his side.

This infuriated Clynes who, in trying to explain the intricacies of his role, was inevitably put on the defence The Labour manifesto proposed nationalising banks, and seeking 'emergency powers' to attain its objectives. This gave the coalition government and its friends in the press the chance to revive the 'Red Scares' of previous elections. The manifesto was attacked by Philip Snowden in a BBC broadcast as 'Bolshevism run mad," finally removing any last vestige of regard he may have had for the party. MacDonald travelled around the country, lambasting Labour for its irresponsibility and raising the spectre of large-scale inflation destroying the value of money, holding up old Weimar Republican Deutschmarks to make the point.1

The Tories also did their best to create an air of panic and spread false rumours to alarm the electorate, such as Steven Runciman's completely false allegation that the previous Labour government had considered raiding people's Post Office savings accounts to raise money. This looked like a coordinated attack on Labours fiscal probity, and was clearly approved by MacDonald with its implication that the savings of so many would be unsafe under a Labour government.

Clynes had never experienced an election campaign so unpleasant, and was genuinely shocked at the 'lies and manipulation of the people.' To hear old colleagues, with whom he had so recently served in cabinet trying to find a solution to mass unemployment, attack and libel the party they had all spent a lifetime supporting was almost more than he could bear. He was incredulous when Snowden made his famous broadcast, with the absurd claim that Labour was more Bolshevik party than a socialist one, and again alleging peoples savings were unsafe under Labour.

Clynes pessimistic about the outcome of the election,

and it was soon clear a heavy defeat or Labour was likely. In Manchester Platting, the Tory Coalition candidate won easily with a majority of 5760 was larger than Clynes had ever enjoyed in the seat. The national result was a landslide for the National Government, and every member of Labour cabinet was defeated except Clynes and Lansbury. Labour lost 235 seats and was reduced to a rump of only 52 MPs. The election, described by the *Manchester Guardian* as 'the shortest, strangest and most fraudulent election of our time,' was a massive defeat with the loss of 2 million voters in a withdrawal of support built up over the past thirty years. The party still attracted six million, mainly working class, votes but electoral system gave them few seats. The government won 556 seats and looked as if it would be in poweror many years.

Only a few Labour MP's followed MacDonald into the new government, standing as 'National Labour' candidates, of whom thirteen were elected these included both MacDonald and his son Malcolm. J.H. Thomas was also elected National Labour, while Snowden resigned to take a peerage. Meanwhile, the Labour Party faced the huge problem of providing an effective opposition, and the task of re-building the popularity of the party in the country with new faces and policies. For the first time in twenty-five years Clynes was no longer an MP and merely an onlooker, but also sad and angry. He was still President of the GMWU, and could devote more time to trade union work, with the hope that a strong trade union movement could provide the basis for Labour's recovery.

Moreover, the trade unions and TUC looked certain to play an important role in reviving the party during what was likely to be a long period in the wilderness. One of the main lessons Clynes took from the whole affair was that the nationalisation of basic industry and the banks was vital if the fate of the economy was never to to be left in the hands of bankers and financiers again. The private sector must never be allowed to dictate policy, and engineer a Labour government's fall in collaboration with a right-wing press. In this he was reasserting his old socialist principles, but now in the light of bitter experience and freed from all the constraints of being in government.2

The Labour Movement had to renew itself, and it was clear that the old Labour Party of the 1920's had been destroyed by the events of 1931. This was not only due to the severe electoral defeat the party had sufered, but also because the older generation were perceived as having failed to advance the prospect of a socialist society. The main culprits may have been MacDonald, Snowden, and Thomas, but all the other members of the 1929-31 government were more or less held responsible, whether they had supported the spending cuts of not. Apart from the 'betrayal' of MacDonald, all of the older generation were considered to have been too concerned with convincing the press and the establishment that the Labour Party was now respectable enough to be trusted with power. But the strategy had failed as millions of the working class continued to vote for the Tories, and Labour had clearly not succeeded increating a mass grassroots support base.

For so long Clynes and his colleagues had supported the strategy, always willing to avoid association with class conflict and pursuing peaceful collaboration. When he led the party into the 1922 election, he spoke of Labour as 'the best bulwark against violent upheaval and class war,' but it begged the question of what the party should do if class war did occur. Its reaction to the 1926 General Strike did seem to show that it would be one of standing aloof, and hoping the problem would be resolved by others. In 1931 when it came to the decisive moment, after much dithering, it sided with the established order.

Although Clynes always had enormous respect for the working class some of his colleagues, notably Snowden and MacDonald, now had a barely concealed contempt, disparaging them for fecklessness and self-indulgence. Clynes felt that the chances of a establishing a socialist society was remote unless the mass of people were firstly converted to the merits of a socialist society. This was a problem handicapping the party since its inception, and it has arguably continued to do so.

In the 1930's Labour began to have some success in reconciling advocacy of public ownership and economic planning with the more conservative instincts of many of its s upporters. Although Clynes always saw the economic role of nationalisation as vital, he and the older generation had never been in the position to implement it. But their underlying commitment to financial orthodoxy would have made it unlikely. At the 1934 TUC conference, Clynes moved a resolution on the 'failure of capitalism' that also suggested the best way to deal with the malign effects of the free market was with frequent government intervention, supplemented by the action of the trade unions to 'humanise' capitalism rather than tame it.

That hardly seems like a commitment to massive state control over swathes of basic industry, and the key may be his belief that nationalisation and central planning should always be legitimized through the ballot box. I this was absent, the best Labour could do in power was ameliorate the worst of the social and economic conditions by benign intervention. His belief in parliamentary sovereignty to protect against 'artificial devices' or or 'the force merely of a parliamentary decision that may not be backed by popular will.' was still largely the same as in 1918.3 In other words, advancing the role of the state should be an evolutionary process, gradually putting into place additional bits of socialism in a piecemeal fashion, and only when the people were convinced of its necessity. The minority Labour governments were ineffective because they did not enjoy sufficient mass support to provide a large majority, and be able to implement a socialist agenda.

In this respect Clynes recognized that Labour could not take public opinion with it towards a democratic socialist future unless the people were convinced of its value. This required a massive effort of education and communication, which Clynes saw as one of the prime functions of the trade unions and the party, hopefully leading to a process of mass conversion that might take decades. There was also a dialogue required between the party leadership, trade unions, the membership and the voters that would require compromise and adjustments to the taste of many. But instead, after its 1931 defeat Labour retreated for a time into tribalist attitudes, a deep suspicion of the leadership, and concern about powerful leaders with too much authority.

In July 1934, the ILP decided to disaffiliate from the party, disillusioned by what what it saw as its drift to the right. This saddened Clynes who had been a founding member of the party, and had retained his membership through many disputes over thirty five years. The ILP had become much less important for recruitment, and its function as the conscience of the Labour Party had been been taken over by the Socialist League. This, under the leadership of Stafford Cripps, provided the intellectual impetus for more left-wing policies, and the formation of a Popular Front against the rise of fascism.

The Communist Party took every opportunity in the 1930's to lead protests against mass unemployment, and attracted more young people. Labour appeared more lethargic, with its aging leadership at both local and national levels, still cautious about involvement with public protests demonstrations and marches. The old fear of being branded subversive, unsound, or crypto-communist by the Tory press, still had an inhibiting effect. Labour even failed to fully endorse the Jarrow hunger marchers in 1936, keeping its distance and even forbidding local constituency party's from giving help and hospitality to them on the southward route to London.

This attitude created a vacuum for other groups on the left to fill, notably the Communist Party. Clynes was still strongly anti-Communist as were the new Labour leadership, and the GMWU still in the forefront of preventing Communist infiltration. But this implacable opposition meant that Labour abdicated the role it should perhaps have played organising mass protests against unemployment, and it developed a fear of involvement with any extra-parliamentary protest that might have included the Communists, but from which it stayed aloof, such as the National Unemployed Workers Movement.

The problem of mass unemployment dominated the early 1930's, and the recommendations of the May report led to the introduction of the 'means test'. By this test total resources were taken into account in the assessing of entitlement to relief payments. This did galvanise the Labour Party into action, and Clynes attacked it on the grounds of its unfairness in that it penalised people who had been thrifty, not significantly because it breached the principle of universal payment of benefits. In a time of austerity this may have been more pragmatic politics, but it hardly indicated a commitment to the universal welfare state.

The hunger marches and protests that were such a feature of the 1930s received no official support from the Labour Party, and protests against the means tests were left to individuals such as James Maxton and Ellen Wilkinson to help organise. The trade unions also were wary of involvement in such protests, concentrating on safeguarding the jobs their members they already had.

This was true of the GMWU and there is no evidence that Clynes had any sympathy for public protests and demonstrations against unemployment or the means tests, although he certainly protested privately. Although the Labour Party did little outside the talking shop of Westminster, local authorities it controlled refused to allow their Public Assistance Committees to follow the new government rules on means testing.

These were soon replaced by the Unemployment Assistance Board in 1934 which attempted to take unemployment assistance out of local politics. But the new assistance rates paid were less than under the old system, and the hunger marches began again. Chamberlain as the Chancellor of the Exchequer was the object of Labour attacks, and there was much conflict over the rates of assistance paid to the unemployed. Although Labour was prepared to oppose the government's policies with vigour in Parliament, it was still hesitant about support extra-parliamentary protests against them.

Now devoting much more time to union affairs, Clynes sought to increase trade union influence within the Labour Party. He had, of course, always seen the unions as the bedrock of the labour movement and a valuable source of recruitment of party personnel. He thought trade union involvement as a way for young people to gain political experience, starting as shop stewards and proceeding to become district and regional officials, and for some to reach national level. He encouraged local shop stewards and officials to get involved in party politics, and to seek election as local councillors and represent labour on all elected bodies, including Trades Councils, borough and county councils, as councillors, magistrates, mayors, and as MPs.

Clynes supported the TUCs efforts to ensure the trade unions had an important influence on Labour policy, and were not just restricted to industrial matters. It could be argued that it was this influence, and the moderation of the trade unions, that helped to keep the Labour Party on the democratic parliamentary road. After the disaster of 1931 there were strong voices in the party arguing the result was evidence that capitalism and the status quo would always triumph, at least under the current constitutional arrangements.

Stafford Cripps and others thought that the next Labour Government should adopt emergency powers to overcome attempts by the House of Lords, the civil service, or other body to frustrate its plans. Cripps saw the 1931 crisis as evidence of capitalism's capacity to overthrow a democratically elected government, using extra-parliamentary methods. He also argued in favour of any future Labour government protecting itself by assuming emergency powers to resist such an attempt happening again. Although Clynes did not have the same contempt for left-wing intellectuals as Ernest Bevin and other trade union leaders, the views of Cripps, Laski and others in the Socialist League were anathema to him and most of the trade union leadership. The influence union leaders helped to keep Labour wedded to the parliamentary path, and well away from the adoption of any plans forfor constitutional reforms.

This was perhaps an omission too far, as it meant there were no further plans to reform the voting system, the House of Lords, or the devolution of any powers to Scotland and Wales. These were issues that would come back in time to haunt Labour. And yet in the 1930s the Party was amazingly complacent and content with the constitution, and the established order in general. It was far less reformist in its intentions than Labour had been previously, when it had various ambitious schemes for constitutional change. Clynes had been an ardent supporter of voting reform in the earlier days, unsurprisingly as Labour had suffered unfairly from the system in 1924, 1929 and 1931, and was to do so again in 1935.

It seems strange that the Party which had been twice recently ejected from power, as a minority government without a safe majority, by party manoeuvring and right wing pressure, should have been so complacent on this issue. But the social conservatism of the new leadership, compared to figures on the intellectual Left such as Cripps, Laski and G.D.H. Cole, was remarkable. Clynes by now shared Bevin's view that demonstrating a readiness for government involved being 'responsible' and consistent, not by adopting new and untried policies, although to others it smacked of a complacency and conservatism.4

There is a distinct impression that people like J.H. Thomas and Clynes, whether they stayed in the Party or not after 1931, had a respect for a system that had enabled them, humble working men from impoverished backgrounds, to rise to ministerial office. It seemed as if the clammy hand of the Establishment had embraced them and left a permanent mark, ensuring their loyalty to the monarchy and the constitution.

Further signs of Clynes's orthodoxy and support for the constitutional status quo are shown in his continued support of the monarchy. He always admired George VI and what he saw as his openness to new political trends, and his readiness to accept changes. Clynes also thought he had provided a focus for stability at a time of rapid change, and was impressed with what he saw as the Kings generosity in accepting into high political office people like himself with origins in manual labour and impoverishment. He always remembered 'the courtesy, sympathy, and helpfulness to us when, with an inevitable degree of uneasiness, we first presented ourselves at the palace as his State advisors.'[5]

Clynes believed his own respect and affection for the monarchy was shared by the rest of the British people, confirmed for him by the crowds who silently lined the streets as George VIs funeral procession passed in 1936, a crowd estimated at over two million people. However, he did not think that deference and respect for established institutions was incompatible at all with democratic socialism of a particular British kind. He did not see the monarchy and the House of Lords, as many on the left did, as both reflecting and reinforcing social inequality and the hierarchical nature of British society, but rather as rocks of stability during a time of change. It was not just the older generation of Labour leaders who held these views, but the newer generation who took over the leadership in the 1930's, such as Morrison, Attlee, and Bevin, who all displayed similar deference to established institutions of the state.

But Clynes took a rather more different stand on the

issues of accepting titles and membership of the House of Lords. He disapproved of both, and admired people who declined titles when offered them, strongly disapproving of the way that MacDonald used his patronage powers in this respect to reward old cronies or bribe his opponents. He himself preferred to remain as an MP, although he could probably have taken a peerage after 1940. At the 1935 Labour Party conference the future of the House of Lords was debated, and despite the criticisms of Harold Laski that it was an an anachronism incompatible with democratic socialism, there was no no interest in either supporting either its abolition or even reform.6

When MacDonald had offered an hereditary peerage to the historian and Christian Socialist, R.H. Tawney, he declined and enquired of the Prime Minister what harm he had done the Labour Party to deserve such an offer. But the leadership, and most of Labour's leaders were were more cynical or complacent, arguing that the party had to be represented there and possibly looking forward to retiring there themselves. Despite this, the party conference passed a resolution disapproving of the acceptance of honours or titles, 'other than those the the Labour Government deems it necessary for the furtherance of its own business in Parliament.'7 The NEC never adopted any proper guidelines for acceptance of honours, and when Attlee became Prime Minister in 1945 he exercised his powers of patronage to the full and created 85 hereditary peerages. Tawney, again made an offer, this time declined with an expression of surprise to Attlee that Labour was still interested in such baubles baubles. Apparently they were, and Attlee himself later accepted a hereditary earldom.8

At first Clynes felt some relief at being free from his parliamentary duties, and having more time to devote to union affairs. But after twenty-five years he missed the House of Commons and some of a MP's privileges, such as walking into the Commons dining-room for lunch without another MP taking him in as a visitor, and the use of the Library, even though as Privy Councillor he could go into the precincts of the Lords. He had a very high boredom threshold, and could sit for hours during debates, or on committees without feeling the tedium He enjoyed feeling part of the institution and its club-like atmosphere that seduced many on the left, helping to dilute their radicalism. He was determined to return at the next election, even though he would then be sixty-six years old, an elder statesman in the party, and dismissed by some as one of the 'old gang' who had failed to stand up to MacDonald.

Clynes was still President of the GMWU, and remained a powerful influence in the union. It had by now become one of the country's largest after a further series of amalgamations, and remained one of the most moderate and conformist of all the unions affiliated to the TUC and the Labour Party. Clynes helped ensure it always an influence for moderation on policy, much to the annoyance of the younger generation. This influence was important because of the 'block vote' at at Labour Party conferences where the trade unions commanded millions of votes which were usually crucially important in the carrying of resolutions. In1930, the GMWU had at its command 250,000 votes, an increase increase over the 200,000 it had in 1925, and they were usually used in favour of moderate resolutions as they had in the 1920s and remained as as its membership continued to grow due to the recovery in employment levels in the 1930s and into the post-war years.

However, the influence of Clynes in the Labour Party had diminished, and the younger generation had come to dominate policy-making. He was not made a member of NEC Policy Committee set up at the end of 1931, which created a policy-making machinery for the first time in the party, but which did include Morrison and Dalton. Clynes liked and admired the latter, who had been friendly and supportive during the dark days of 1930-31.

Hugh Dalton was an Old Etonian, former economics lecturer at the LSE, and had been a junior minister. He was an ambitious and assiduous networker, serving as the NEC representative on the Economic Committee of the TUC General Council, that became the liaison link between the unions and the NEC Policy Committee. He key figure in the Labour revival of the 1930's, and it was largely due to Dalton that 'planning' became the key to all future Labour policies. Dalton became an 'intellectual' on the party executive,' and his biographer makes clear that the Labour Party that entered the wartime coalition in1940, and formed the government five years later wore the indelible mark of Dalton's influence.9 This had the approval of Clynes who he always supported policy planning that took trade union views into account. They were impressed by Soviet economic planning, as well as new Keynesian economic theories that that began percolating into party policy discussions through such bright young intellectuals as Douglas Jay.There was now much more emphasis on the collection of economic data, and ideas about 'managing' the macroeconomy.

There was also a slow recovery in the morale of the Labour Party under the leadership of George Lansbury, who had succeeded Henderson, with Clement Attlee as his deputy. There were by-election successes, and some of those defeated in 1931 returned as MPs, although most of the leading younger leading figures, such as Dalton and Herbert Morrison, had to wait until 1935 to return. But the sheer lack of MPs meant that the Labour Party in Parliament was inevitably marginalised between 1931 and 1935. Despite the by-election successes, there was a feeling that the party would be unlikely to win the next election as circumstances were favourable to the government.

Economic conditions improved with a rise in real wages, lower interest rates, and an increase in house building, that seemed to indicate recovery from the depression. As the 1935 general election approached, the Conservatives began warning the electorate that voting Labour risked undermining this fragile recovery and cause another economic crisis. But there were also underlying changes taking place that were favourable to Labour, notably a younger generation of voters who were experiencing the hardships of unemployment, and as a result becoming more politicized than their parents.

Clynes remained politically active, speaking around the country at large and small meetings. He was increasingly concerned with the issue of disarmament, as he believed an arms race inevitably led to war, and wanted Labour to pledge to end the private manufacture of armaments. The Labour leadership realised this might be an issue which could help drive a wedge between the public and the Government, and help the party revival. The issue was regularly raised by speakers in by-election campaigns between 1931 and 1935, with both Margaret Bondfield and Herbert Morrison addressing it at the by-election at Skipton, and Clynes at Harborough in 1932 speaking of the Labour Party now 'preaching ceaselessly the gospel of peace. We are an unqualified peace party.10

The advocacy of peace and disarmament seemed at this stage a useful vote-winner, and chimed in with the inclinations of many in the party, especially Lansbury who had been a committed pacifist from his early days in the ILP. But as the threat from the Mussolini's policy of expansion grew, so did support for collective security in the party, that included Dalton and Bevin, although Clynes still was reluctant.

By 1934 the party was trying to detach itself from pacifism, and embrace collective security. At the Annual Conference that year, a resolution was proposed in favour of supporting collective security against foreign aggression, which was adopted. George Lansbury was in hospital and unable to attend the conference or the NEC meeting, but his pacifist views were well known. He would have opposed the policy the as being likely to lead

to war. Despite the increasing threat to the peace from
Nazi Germany and Fascist Italy, at the 1935 conference
Lansbury made his opposition to collective security clear,
and strongly opposed a resolution supporting sanctions
against Mussolini. There a brutal attack on Lansbury by
Ernest Bevin, who took the trade union line that all
collective agreements should be respected above any
issues of conscience. Clynes supported Lansbury on this
this matter, but it was a personal view and opposed to
the majority trade union line. However, Lansbury felt he
had no option but to resign and Clement Attlee took
over as leader. Clynes was aghast at this internal party
strife, although he was coming to see the dangers of
drifting into war unarmed and unprepared. And soon he
came round to support the majority view in the labour
movement that the only way to stop the aggression of
the dictators was by collective sanctions.

In the general election campaign of 1935 the Tory
Prime Minister, Stanley Baldwin, portrayed himself as a
bastion of steady common sense and the epitome of
moderation at a time of growing international tension.
The Tories painted Labour as irresponsible and not to
be trusted with either foreign policy or the fragile econ-
mic recovery. In Manchester, Clynes fought a vigorous
campaign, and detected enough disillusionment with the
National Government to hope for success. Elsewhere
in the country there was indeed a large swing to Labour
of over 7%, but as usual with the electoral system it
this did not translate into seats. The Labour Party won

won 154 seats, a gain of 105 with almost 8 million votes. The Conservatives won 387 seats, with over ten million votes, the National Liberals obtained 44 seats, and the Liberals 161. The National Government parties, however, enjoyed a total of 54% of the vote compared to Labour's 38%. For Labour there was consolation in recovering two-thirds of the support it lost in 1931, and in seeing MacDonald easily defeated by Manny Shinwell at Seaham Harbour.

The best results were in London, which became a Labour parliamentary stronghold to match its local government strength. But in the North and in Scotland the recovery was patchy and partial. Clynes was elected in straight fight with the Conservatives, but with a small majority. But he was glad enough to be returned with a majority of just a thousand votes. The result was:

J.R. Clynes (Lab):	1,353
J.W. Stansfield (Con):	17,013
Maj :	1337

He was pleased to be back in Parliament and welcome as a popular 'elder' statesmen of the party and forgiven, although not by all, for the 'great betrayal' of 1931. His reputation was still such that he was invited to contest the party leadership elections in October 1935, perhaps more as a gesture of affection than of evidence of any serious chance of success, although some would have liked him to have the chance so narrowly denied in 1922. There was a desire to continue with a more emollient

leader, but Clynes declined because he knew his time for
leadership had passed, and there were several younger
able candidates available. Attlee was elected, and Clynes
was glad to have the greater freedom of being a back-
bencher, even though his contributions were always as
measured and moderate as ever. Once his critics had
mocked himfor his inaction - 'when in doubt do nowt'-
or as one who usually 'de-Clyned' to take action, but
experience had taught him the dangers of hastening to
judgement, and to listen carefully before making up his
mind. So he was seen regularly attending debates where
he listened carefully, especially in foreign affairs which
came to dominate the next few years.

10
Recovery to Victory

From 1935 Labour was a more substantial opposition in Parliament, although it still faced a National Coalition Government with a large majority, now thoroughly dominated by the Tories. Attlee proved a more ambitious and ruthless leader than many in the party suspected, especially those such as Beatrice Webb who had dismissed him as a 'little nonentity'. He believed in delegation and team work, but his shadow cabinet colleagues were never in any doubt where authority lay.

The issue of rearmament and collective security became pressing as Nazi Germany and Fascist Italy were becoming increasingly beligerant. The invasion of Abyssinia by Italian forces showed the dangers of relying on collective security alone, although the National Government was still ready to concede to Mussolini what he wanted. The same occurred when the Spanish civil war began, and instead of pledging support to the Republicans in the fight to defend democracy, they were left alone to face the Nationalist forces. Despite initially supporting the National Government's non-intervention policy from 1935, Labour gradually shifted away towards facing the reality of military aggression and the need for rearmament.

But this was not an easy process, and Clynes was among many in the Party who continued to support disarmament and failed to see the Nazi menace early on for what it was. It was one thing to argue that rearmament in defence of democracy was unjustified, but quite another to allow unrestricted imperial expansion by a fascist state intent on crushing democracy. In this respect he was one of the many in all political parties who failed to see the dangers posed by Hitler, and like most that had lived through the First World War was understandably loath to live through another.

The public also apparently preferred peace, and at the East Fulham by-election in 1933 a Tory majority of 7000 was overturned by a Labour candidate considered to be anti-war. A Peace Ballot organised by the League of Nations in 1934 resulted in a majority in favour of collective security. These indicators encouraged the disarmers, including Clynes, but by 1936 the situation was changing rapidly. The Abyssinian crisis had revealed the threat to Britain's imperial interests and national security, and from 1937 the Labour Party voted for increased military spending in the House of Commons. At the Party conference that year, the policy of non-intervention in Spain was reversed to one of openly supporting the Republican cause. This was partly in response to the enormous sympathy for that cause among party members and on the left generally, although, apart from the volunteers in the International Brigade, it mainly took the form of organising humane aid.

The idea of a Popular Front against fascism was increasingly discussed in Left wing circles by1936, led by

Hugh Dalton and G.D.H. Cole, who were influenced by the formation of the Popular Fronts in both France and Spain, which were an effort to present a common front of the Left against the threat of fascism. It was argued that after the disappointment of 1935, Labour would be unable to form a government again unless there was a unity between all the centre-left forces in British politics, including the Liberals, Communists, the uncommitted or and even liberal Tories. But to Clynes, and many others in the Labour Party, the idea of making common cause with the Communists was anathema, having spent so long combating their influence in the trade union movement. Besides, he thought they would use the common front to advance their own agenda, that did not include a commitment to any sort of democratic socialism.

The appeal of a Popular Front was then superseded by the United Front campaign promoted by Stafford Cripps and the Socialist League, with the idea of including the ILP and Communists in common cause with Labour. Again, Clynes opposed this for the same reasons he had the Popular Front, although this plan had wider support in the Party. In any case, the NEC would have nothing to do with it although Cripps was re-elected to the NEC where he formed a left-wing group with EllenWilkinson, Harold Laski and D.N. Pritt. Although the NEC tried to impose its views on the wider party membership, there was continuing support for some kind of common cause against fascism in cooperation with other parties of the centre and left at constituency level. This became more urgent with the growth in the activities of the British Union of Fascists led by Oswald Mosley. In the London constituency of Lambeth North, the party accepted help from the Communists at elections, organising aid for the Spanish Republicans and supporting a common front. It supported the local MP, George Strauss, who was an ally of Herbert Morrison on the LCC, although it soon led to the North Lambeth CLP being suspended from the main national party for a time.1

The activities of the British Union of Fascists under Mosley were deeply alarming to the Left in general, and Clynes was deeply saddened to see the political direction in which Mosley had moved. Although always suspicious of his previous cabinet colleague, Clynes had nevertheless admired his energy and commitment to ending the unemployment problem, even if his rhetoric always seemed to be excessive and his egocentric vanity was a match for MacDonald. The violence displayed at the BUF Olympia rally and in the 'battle' of Cable Street in East London led to the passing of the Public Order Act in 1937. The law banned the wearing of political uniforms in public places or meetings, and training for usurping the police or or military. Clynes welcomed the Act on the grounds it represented only a minor threat to civil liberty, and was specifically aimed against fascism. 'A garb answers to a uniform and worn in what really is a military march and in a manner and spirit brings into our political activities alien elements making for conflict and disorder.'2

Mass unemployment continued to persist in industrial areas, and although the economy was starting to recover. Labour was prepared to criticize the government for its lack of effective policies. It produced plans, some of them radical, for solving the problem which included targeted public expenditure based on Keynesian principles. But it was less comfortable supporting a large well-publicised demonstration such as the march of the unemployed from Jarrow to London in 1936. The Left tried to commit the Labour Party more radically to the cause of the unemployed through the Jarrow March, and combat the Communist Party's efforts in local organisation of the unemployed and it's use of mass unemployment for the propaganda.

The Labour Party parliamentary leadership remained wary of associating the party with campaigning outside parliamentary, including protests of the unemployed. The local constituency Labour parties were asked not to give any assistance or hospitality to the Jarrow marchers, that Ellen Wilkinson the local Labour MP, had helped to organise. Several Labour-controlled local authorities on the route of the march, however, ignored the instruction, providing food and sleeping facilities for marchers.

When the marchers reached Parliament Square in London, no official Labour Party representatives were willing to meet with them, although individual Labour MPs did so. The police did their best to provoke public disorder by forcing the marchers to disperse down King William Street towards Victoria. Clynes, as ever, was pulled between sympathy for the unemployed and belief in the maintenance of public order and , as in 1926, fear that Labour would be associated with militancy and disorder. So he remained, staying firmly on the House green benches and only saw the marchers as he made his way to and from the tube station to the Commons.

By now Clynes was one of the longest serving Labour MPs in the House, and although respected as such on all sides of the Chamber, seemed increasingly opposed to anything that appeared to threaten the status quo. By now the 'parliamentary embrace' appeared to have enveloped him, and he was a stout defender of it's traditions and conventions. A stickler for parliamentary procedure, the courtesies of the place, and its club-like atmosphere suited his personality. He knew that when he spoke he would be listened to in respectful silence, although he spoke very rarely and preferred to listen in silence to the debates through the long afternoons. In his late sixties now, he had already been an MP for twenty-eight years by 1936, and had lived through all the dramatic events of the century knew well many of the leading participants including Churchill and Lloyd George, who were of course also still in the House of Commons

This love of parliamentary institutions lay to some extent in wonder and awe at being in the place at all given his humble origins. Instead of this making him question these institutions, and their possible isolation from the people, it had the reverse effect as he got older, making him even more respectful of them. This kind of institutional conservatism was common among many of the older Labour members, their sclerosis more or less complete by 1930, with Clynes the longest survivor of that generation. Most had favoured reform of the House of Lords and the voting system in their younger days, and had even entertained republican ideas. Clynes had advocated all of these as a younger man, in addition to opposing capital punishment. But by now all of these of these opinions had been reversed, and from the 20's his patriotism and deference were more pronounced.

The argument, as usual, was the need for Labour to be seen to support established institutions of the state, including the monarchy, given its vulnerability to charges of disloyalty and the huge popularity of the monarchy as an institution. It was was also linked to the issue of patriotism, and the fear in the Labour Party of being smeared as unpatriotic. This had more influence with the newer generation of Labour leaders, and was illustrated most dramatically in the abdication crisis that erupted in December 1936.

When the new King, Edward VIII, wanted the law changed to permit him to marry a commoner, Baldwin refused, but consulted Attlee as the Leader of the Opposition. Attlee took the view, which Clynes shared, that a royal marriage was not just a personal issue for those involved, but also a public and constitutional one and the King should accept the constitutional advice he was given. It was completely impossible, in their view, for the the King to marry Mrs Simpson, a commoner, and that the private lives of monarchs, like politicians and other public figures, were circumscribed by their position and responsibilities, and they could not act as if they were private citizens. The nation was divided, as the young King was popular, and after his abdication one result was a demand for the abolition of the monarchy entirely by some sections of the Left.

Apart from approving the existing monarchical system, Clynes thought that if Labour got into a controversy over the monarchy it would backfire badly and cause the party electoral damage. If it went further, and adopted a more extreme republican stance it would be even worse:

> These voices are those of troubled souls crying in the wilderness and hoping against hope to be noticed. They represent neither British Labour nor the Parliamentary Labour Party. So long as the throne remains loyal to the constitution, British Labour remains loyal to the throne.2

In reality it was Attlee, Baldwin, Clynes and the whole political establishment that was out of touch with public opinion, and a large number of people supported the royal marriage on the grounds that the King had a right to marry the woman he loved. If Labour had backed the King, the government would have split and Baldwin might have resigned. But Clynes was 'no supporter of the fulsome adulation of monarchs - I think it ridiculous,' and had no time for court ceremonial or attempts to invest royalty with mystique.3 But he was still a staunch supporter of the institution of monarchy, and as a privy councillor felt pleased to serve on the committee that organised George Vs coronation.

In 1937 Clynes published his memoirs in two volumes and, as with most political autobiographies, they adopted a rather self-justificatory tone with a good bit of score settling, but they alos contained poignant chapters on his childhood poverty and youthful struggles, and provide graphic insight into the struggle for self-education of the talented urban working class in the later years of the nineteenth century. He also conveyed well the atmosphere of confusion and disillusionment in the last days of the second Labour government, as MacDonald walked away from the party he once loved.

As foreign affairs increasingly came to dominate the political agenda, Labour was able to reflect the popular feeling more about resistance to the threat of German and Italian aggression. Clynes was more reconciled to the acceptance of re-armament in order to be ready for the what looked like an imminent war, and he approved the TUC assertion in April 1937 that to play a full role in collective security, rearmament could not be dispensed with. He also joined other Labour MPs, in voting for increased military expenditure from 1937, although the leadership was still prevaricating on the issue. The party's repositioning contrasted with that of the government and and after Chamberlain succeeded Baldwin the policy of appeasement became even stronger. But Popular Front supporters remained very active, and still enjoyed much support amount among the Labour CLP members.

There were complaints about the weak leadership of Attlee, while Chamberlain travelled to Munich to sign a non-aggression agreement with Germany in 1938. In a by-election at Oxford in October 1938 the candidate for Labour candidate opposed by an Independent candidate, A.D. Lindsay, supported by the local Labour Popular

Front dissident group including Richard Crossman, and FrankPakenham. And another Independent supported by the Popular Front won a by-election at Bridgewater.

Ever the party loyalist, and abhorring all this disunity, Clynes opposed the Popular Front movement, staying loyal to the official party line, even though this was unp-among many local party members and voters. Cripps was then dramatically expelled from the Party with several of his supporters from the Popular Front including Strauss and Trevelyan for breaching discipline. There had to be some resolution of the situation and at the Labour Party Annual Conference at Southport in May 1939 the issue came to a head when the confirmation of the expulsion But by the time of the Nazi invasion of Poland, Labour was fully behind the pro-war movement, and there was strong pressure on the NE to have nothing to do with Chamberlain's appeasement policies. Most of the Labour parliamentary party, including Clynes, was behind Attlee in support of the war, and of entering into a coalition government in case of war. Some leading Labour figures like Dalton were less enthusiastic, recalling Henderson's unhappy experience as a cabinet minister during the First World War. But Clynes had only happy memories of working in the wartime cabinet, and considered a gov-ernment of national unity the only way for an effective war to be waged, especially on the home Front.

Finally, Chamberlain reluctantly took the country to war in September 1938. Although Labour was supportive it retained the right to criticize the government, and retained the right to criticize the government refused to join a coalition led by Chamberlain. This contributed to the weakening of Chamberlain's premiership in the nine months of the so-called 'phoney war'. These were very dramatic events that Clynes observed from the backbencches recalling the events leading up to entry into the First World War and the immediate aftermath. He was in the crowded House of Commons for the debate on the conduct of the war, with many members aware of the lack of preparedness of the British army, and with the considerable anger directed at Chamberlain and towards his government for this lack of planning.

When Chamberlain invited Attlee to join a coalition government on 9 May 1939 he refused, and at Labour's conference in Bournemouth, the NEC voted against joining any coalition led by Chamberlain. Chamberlain resigned to be succeeded by Churchill who became the Prime Minister on 23 May. The way was now open for Labour to join a coalition, and after the Churchill met Attlee and Arthur Greenwood, the posts for new Labour ministers were agreed with little disagreement. There was some feelings of resentment in the Labour ranks over joining a government led by Churchill, given his record of dealing with strikes and a view by so many of him as a warmonger and an imperialist. However, Clynes rather liked Churchill on a personal basis, and his knowledge of him went back to the 1900's when they stood together as parliamentary candidates, and had with good humour kicked off a football match at Old Trafford. In any case, the critical situation in the war overrode all other feeling, while Clynes thought the best war leader was needed to be of the government for the duration irrespective of party political rivalries.

These dramatic political events ended with the formal creation of the Coalition Government in May1940, and for the rest of the war Labour was closely associated with the pursuit of victory and preparations for peace. Attlee and Dalton, in particular, had played a skilful game, maximising their opportunities to bring down the Chamberlain government and prepare the way for Labours own inclusion. With Attlee and Greenwood in the war cabinet, and Dalton, Morrison and Bevin as ministers it represented a remarkable recovery from the nadir of the party's fortunes in the mid-1930's. But without the crisis of imminent war, it is doubtful that Labour would have won the election due to have taken place in 1940. In any case, that election was cancelled, and the parliament elected in 1935 continued through to 1945 and the war's end.

The German invasion of Belgium and France, and the greater threat of espionage and spying that arose as a result, saw the proposal for a new law establishing a offence of treachery which carried the death sentence. Some thought the existing legislation covered acts of treason, but the war conditions placed even abolitionists in a difficult moral dilemma. They could have opposed the new law on the same grounds they had in peacetime, as did the Labour MP Sydney Silverman, or accept the or as a moral during a time of extreme national crisis. In the Commons debate Clynes, a lifelong abolitionist, was inclined to adopt the latter argument on the basis that the the death penalty was morally justified in wartime for acts of treason defined as 'tendencies, conspiracies and movements' that were of a type totally unknown to us in all previous conflicts.' He considered 'treachery against one's own country one of the most abominable crimes any man can commit, an enormity. Such a hideous thing to do that, for my part, I'm ready to set aside principles on questions of general capital punishment.' The bill was easily carried into law, despite some vigorous opposition from a few abolitionists, and as a result sixteen people were to be shot by firing squad or hanged for treachery.4

The formation of the Coalition Government was a heartening event to Clynes, seeing Labour once again at the centre of political affairs, and pursuing the national interest on a consensual basis with the other parties. It meant that the party could be seen by the people in a patriotic mode during the hostilities, and there could be now be no doubt about Labour's patriotic credentials that could carry over into the peace.

The hard reality of war soon reached the home front, and rationing was introduced on the 8 January 1940, and bacon, butter, and sugar were put on ration, with ration books issued to all households. A typical weekly ration would only be one egg, 4 oz of margarine, 4 oz of bacon bacon, 2 oz butter and tea. This brought back memories of the First War for Clynes when he was responsible for rationing. His advice was now valued and listened to with respect in debates, and in advice he gave the Ministry of Food. He pointed out the lessons he had learned in the

1917-18 such as the need for consistency in order to
' ...avoid rationing food which a little later they unration,
and later on re-ration. These changes tend to create
irritation in the public mind and make people wonder
how the job is being done'.5

He realised that there were important differences
between the two conflicts. In 1914 the Government had
only reluctantly set up the Food Ministry after shortages
and enormous queues appeared, with the prospect of
civil unrest as a consequence. In the current conflict the
government was more prepared, and could use the
experience from the previous war, but Clynes was also
aware of the difficulties facing the Food Ministry after
1940, especially in regard to foreign food supplies and
the very heavy losses of merchant ships to German U-
Boat attack.

He also knew how important the supply of food was
for domestic morale, and how close the country had
come in the First World War 'to losing it because of
lack of food.' Ensuring the food supply was vital and the
main function of the Food Ministry should be 'the buying
of food, sharing it out fairly, and keeping down the price
of it.'6 The food rationing programme showed that the
important lessons of maintaining adequate food stocks,
dietary advice, issuing additional nutrients to the most
vulnerable, and the close co-ordination of the Ministries
ry of Agriculture and the Central Office of Information
had all been learned.The latter make some most effective
propaganda and information films about preparing food,
avoiding waste, dietary matters, and 'digging for victory.'

By 1942 more problems with rationing had become apparent, familiar to Clynes from the previous conlict, especially in regard to black market trading. This grew considerably as the war progressed and shortages of all became apparent, especially luxuries goods. Eventually, there was a black market in all rationed foodstuffs as well as luxuries like whisky and wine, which although not rationed were in short supply with high prices. There was widespread indignation among people about this, and Clynes advised a coordinated effort to track down and punish miscreants whose crimes 'in my view amount to treason.' he felt in war that 'the worse criminals are those who run the black market and have deliberately organised exploitation in order the make fortunes out of war conditions.'[7] If rationing was to be tolerable it had to be seen as fair and equable for only then would the people see its value and purpose.

The Second World War for most of the people was a just and patriotic conflict, fought to defend democracy from the threat of fascism. It was a total war, fought to the finish with no compromise or vacillation. Clynes had strong satisfaction in seeing the whole nation united in fighting the war, with the very survival of the nation at stake. All MPs stayed in London during the conflict, including the Blitz of 1940 and all the bombing raids that followed. It was a stark reminder of the changed nature of modern war since the previous conflict, and how greater the suffering experienced by a modern urban civilian population. The House of Parliament were not exempt and between 1940 and 1941 both chambers sat in Church House in Westminster, due to the threats from

bombing while they were in session. This threat became a
a realty with raids on the 26 September and 8 December
1940 in which bombs caused damage. There was further
bomb damage and then, on 10-11 May 1941, the House
of Commons Chamber was entirely destroyed by fire and
the roof of the member's lobby collapsed, although
Westminster Hall was saved. Clynes continued to attend
the Commons sessions at Church Hall, carrying his gas
to and from Westminster and joining the crowded trains
home in the evenings to Putney.

All sections of labour were involved on the home
front, with the Labour Party, Trades Councils and the
Co-operative Party seeking representation on the Area
Councils, set up by the Ministry of Supply, and also on
other committees to protect the workers interests. As he
had been involved with this kind of work in the First
War, Clynes hoped this time it would lead to a better
reward for the people after the peace. Although party
politics was put into cold storage for the duration, in the
hope of preparing for the peace, the various local and
national organisations of the Labour Party continued as
in peacetime, including holding annual conferences, even
though it was not able to contest any by-elections that
occurred.

In the House of Commons Labour was in a difficult
position as it had dual role to play, part of the coalition
government, and also having to serve as the official opposition. So tat while it was subject to criticism about the
conduct of the war on both the home and foreign frontsit
also had to be critical of the government of which it also
was a part. Clynes by temperament did not find this a

difficulty and, although not speaking often, he made contributions striving to be both constructive and non-partisan. However, he was prepared to be critical where questions of fairness and equity on the home front were involved, on subjects such as improved training or work opportunities for the disabled and working conditions in mills and factories.

The party political truce was frustrating to many in the Labour Party, especially on the left, and any opportunity to break out of the consensus was welcomed. When the Beveridge Report was published in December 1942, it was avidly discussed in local constituency branches as a basis for a post-war welfare state. It seemed to provide a blueprint for creating a comprehensive system to replace the piecemeal provisions for unemployment, ill-health, and poverty. The response of the Cabinet to the report was far less enthusiastic, and when it was debated in the Commons in February 1943 ninety-nine Labour MPs voted for its early implementation. Clynes was one of these who thought there was no justice or point in waiting until the war was over. He never liked Ernest Bevin particularly his bombastic political style, which was reinforced when he lost his temper in a meeting of PLP and threatened to resign over the implementation of the Beveridge Report proposals. When it was debated at the 1943 Labour conference, Barbara Betts, (later Castle) famously complained it was always 'jam yesterday and jam tomorrow!' But Attlee shared Bevin's view that impleneting the report was putting the cart before the horse, and that all resources should be devoted to the task of winning the war.8

Instead, Clynes had to show his hopes for the future in debates over bills introduced by the government, or piecemeal improvements such as the employment of disabled people. In a debate on this Bill in December 1943, Clynes said how he hoped that current sacrifices being made by the people would lead to a better future for all, and that 'however great be the glory, however great be the record of a country, that will not pay the rent; therefore we must see that some of thesubstance, as well as some of the splendour of the results, may be placed at the feet of those who have done so much to earn it.'9 Not surprisingly he also voted or an increase in the state pensions in April 1943 with sixty one others, mainly Labour MPs.

Meanwhile travelling up and down to his Manchester constituency in wartime could be difficult. There were still scheduled services from Euston station, but the trains were often delayed and overcrowded with troops in transit and other military personnel. The blackout was enforced, and there were often long delays due to essential war materials being carried by rail which often had priority right of way. Poorly heated carriages and poor catering made the journey in wintertime, especially when it snowed, even worse.

When Clynes arrived at Manchester Piccadilly station he centre of the city was a sight of devastation after the blitz of 22-23 December 1940. This caused considerable damage to the centre of the city, with many of the fine old Victorian buildings destroyed or damaged including the Royal Exhange, Manchester Cathedral, Corporation Street and Piccadilly Gardens. By 1941 the people of city were also severely affected by the war with the bomb damage to housing and factories, and food and other shortages. The local Labour Party saw the loss in falling membership, with people serving overseas or in other military capacities at home, and local subscriptions were not being collected due to lack of volunteers.

The electoral truce was also frustrating, by which Labour could not contest by-elections against the Tories. Instead, they saw the newly formed left-wing Common Wealth Party win Tory seats, often with former Labour MPs as candidates, and there were efforts by Aneuran Bevan and others to end this truce, but the proposal was was defeated. Although he understood this frustration, Clynes did not believe that Labour was losing popularity by being in the coalition government, quite the reverse and that they would collect their political reward sooner or later and would be all the greater. He thought people would turn to Labour because he sensed the war had released a desire for radical change and a new start.

By 1944 victory seemed increasingly in sight, and it was only a matter of time before the war ended. There were stirrings within the Labour Party to prepare for the peace, first at grass roots level where local parties were already starting to select candidates for the next general election, and with more critical attacks against sitting Tory MPs who had been appeasers in the 1930's. This new willingness to criticize was also found nationally in the NEC and at Labour Party conferences where it was possible to hold minister to account. There were also those in the party who thought there had been too much consensus and non-partisan coalition building, and the time had now arrived for party politics to resume even before the end of hostilities.9 But Clynes an elder of the party, held himself aloof from these debates, and from all Smoking Room intrigues that had started again in the House of Commons. He had decided the time had come to retire, and to stand down at the next General Election when it came.

The reasons for the Labour's landslide victory in 1945 have been much discussed. The election had been long anticipated, the campaign was well planned and prepared. Most of the candidates had already been chosen, even if some had been selected before being demobilised, while others even turned up to their selection meetings still in uniform. An egalitarian spirit had been fostered in the armed forces and at home, with the feeling that a return to the pre-war social and economic norms was untenable. They had had been been listening to radio programmes during the war, such as the *Brains Trust*, and broadcasters such as Julian Huxley, Cyril Joad, and J.B. Priestley who all raised issues about why the war had been fought, and the kind of society that should be built in the future. The forces vote was important, and probably went largely to Labour, while the Army Bureau of Current Affairs under the auspices of the Army Education Corps played a key by providing discussion forums. Many serving in the forces were angry at the low pay, inadequacy of the preparations for combat, the hierarchical nature of the services, made worse by the peceived incompetence of many officers.10

Clynes finally stood down after thirty five years as a Manchester MP, and watched his first general election for all those years as a spectator. The vote took place on the 5 July 1945, two months after VE Day, and in his old seat at Manchester Platting, Hugh Delargy was chosen as the candidate retained the seat easily with a majority of 7,165, far larger than Clynes had ever enjoyed, and a sign of the changed atmosphere. But he had always been confident that Labour would win, perhaps more so than many in the party fort the landslide was far from expected, and a genuine surprise. Absorbed in the war and in the world of Westminster, it escaped many how a spirit of egalitarianism had spread during the conflict, a war in which everyone had been expected to suffer equally the same privations in in the cause of victory.

Labour also had a more honourable record in regard to standing up to Nazi Germany, and even its pacifist wing did not detract from this. This contrasted with the Tories, a number of whom were tainted by support for either or even support for Nazi Germany, with several of their MPs having links with fascist organizations. However, it is not likely there had been a mass conversion to socialism, but rather a case of turning to Labour to implement extensive but limited aims desired by the majority of the people after the exhausting war was over. The warnings of Clynes and others that the mass conversion of the electorate was still needed before a full socialist revolution remained true.

The Labour landslide of 1945 was more the result of the war and a determination among people not to revert to pre-war social and economic conditions after the sacrifices that had been made. The experience of state involvement in the economy had re-assured them that central planning and state resource allocation were not to be feared, and could deliver benefits for all more effectively than free markets could or would. It involved controls of all kinds which, although accepted in wartime were only tolerable for a short time afterwards. But Clynes's experience with food rationing in 1917 still convinced him that the benefits of controls could be extended into the peace, even covering wages and prices as well as delivering the services of the welfare state.

The election campaign was short, but the turn out high at 73 per cent, far more than the 59% in 1918, which was some evidence of greater politicization of the electorate. In addition, there was less social deference in 1945 which the Second World War helped to reduce, unlike the First. It was clear that the people wanted a better world with good housing and health care, welfare reform and full employment. The Labour manifesto had a focus on these priorities, and it caught the zeitgeist of the moment which carried it to victory with a large majority. When the result was announced on 26 July 1945, after a three week hiatus so that all the votes of the servicemen still overseas could be counted. Labour had won 393 seats, a majority of 180, and the party now represented a majority of the people, with a mandate to create a new kind of society.

It was of course a moment to savour, and a gratifying end for Clynes's political career. It had been a long road since 1900, and he had been on the journey every step of the way, and was now the last real representative of those early pioneers who crowded into Farringdon Hall to form the Labour Representation Committee. It was possible for the party to implement plans that Clynes could hardly

have envisaged in his early political life. He tended to see
politics as a calling rather than a profession, almost semi-
religious in its nature. It was the cause of socialism that
mattered more than personal preferment or gratification.
He had stuck to this belief all his adult life, and it kept
him going through all the setbacks. He felt that:

> Labour serves the British people because it is a movement *of*
> the people. We have faced the people's problems ourselves,
> in our own home and in the humble homes of our parents...
> Many of us have found in political life, not a splendid career,
> but an expression of our religion. A position has not been
> viewed as a job but as a Cause.11

However, he had not been retired long when the were
personal problems with which to contend. In 1943 his
wife, Mary, had been injured during an air raid, had been
unwell for some time and was now an invalid with more
medical problems. The only income they had was £6 per
week pension from his trade union into which he paid for
many years. He had never thought much about his likely
financial situation in retirement, and probably never had
an expectation that he would be in relative poverty during
old age. It is unsurprising that he felt some resentment
about this, and wrote a letter to the *The Times* outlining the
injustice of his situation. This must have been difficult,
but in a long political and union career he had worked
hard to improve the lives of others, and now found himself left in near penury. He also wanted to protest the lack
of proper pensions for MPs and ex-Cabinet ministers that
hit Labour people particularly hard, with no private means
or other source of income. They often found themselves

in penurious circumstances in retirement or after defeat in an election.17

The Clynes semi-detached house in St John's Road, off Putney Hill in South West London, was quite large and comfortable, but the maintenance costs were high and Mary's medical costs mounted. The new National Health Service was not yet in operation, and they had no private health insurance. There was an MP's fund into which all sitting MP's paid £12 a year, as had Clynes. An ex-MP in financial difficulties he could apply for help, but these amounts were not large, and only available to those in the direst the need. They were almost always made available as 'one-off' amounts, and in any case application was limited to those with incomes below £4 a week. The letter to *The Times* did lead to the setting up of a fund by the PLP for MPs, and articles followed in the press arguing the case for and against the proposal of pensions for MPs.

The Spectator was sympathetic to Clynes's predicament, describing him as 'one of the very best type of Labour Members,' and going on to describe how ' he has been left at 77 with an invalid wife and income of £6 a week.' But it still went on to argue against pensions for MP's and ex-ex-cabinet ministers, and that it should be up to Clynes's trade union or the Labour Party to provide further help.17

After this, a special fund was collected by MP's for him, butthe last years of Clynes's life were not spent in much comfort . Yet he could take heart as he saw the Labour government carry out its programme to set up a welfare state, create a National Health Service, and nationalise the coal industry and the railways. He was grateful to have lived to see it, and amazed at the pace of the changes. It was a justification for the faith that had sustained the pioneers in the early days of the struggle when 'collarless moneyless, and almost wordless, earnestly believed that it was wrong for the ill-educated to be exploited for the benefit of aristocrats. We were prepared to die for our faith knowing that others would come after us to whom our failing hands would throw the torch.'14

Clynes's died on 23 October 1949, and cremated at Putney Vale. Clement Attlee, the Prime Minister, paid a fulsome tribute in the House of Commons, and after out-lining his various roles went on to say that 'it will be said of him that he never made an enemy. I think his outstanding quality was his complete unselfishness and his complete loyalty ....But I think of him as a very likeable perosn. One could never meet him without realising how how kind, how unassuming he was...' then Anthony Eden recalled his modesty and sincerity and Clement Davies, who known him for forty-four years, recalled his shy diffidence, but also hid his abilities, determination, and strength of conviction.15

There is no blue plaque on the house in Putney to-day, nor on any building in Oldham or Manchester. And Clynes would not have been concerned by this for to serve the cause was reward enough, and his memorial the improvement in the lives of the working poor. It had been a long run for the poor boy from Oldham, small and unassuming, who forced himself despite shyness to become a public speaker and debater. Clynes may have lacked the charisma and vocal powers of MacDonald, nor been able to sway the House of Commons or large crowds in the same way. He was an organiser, unifier and strategist who put the interests of the working class above personal ambition or party intrigue.

In 1940 Clynes contributed to a series of war pamphlets intended to bolster morale at home, covering the reasons for the war and the sacrifices being made. In *When I Remember,* Clynes recalled as a small boy running barefoot on the oily cotton mill floor, and contrasted this with the many improvement he had seen in his lifetime achieved 'not with a sweep of magic wand' but largely by the 'courage, patience and sincerity of a band self-educated visionaries in red ties and baggy trousers.' Too modest to say so, but he had been one them in the endless meetings, speeches, and elections, he was always trying to create a mass movement for social change.

He was surveying these changes in 1940, at a time when the war seemed far from won, and the prospect of a post-war socialist government a remote possibility. He ended with a paragraph that could just as well have been his own epitaph nine years later, which read:

> I recall once more the earlier days of my Trade Union work. When we were struggling to build up for th people of this country a decent standard of living with some sense of status and dignity. When i remeber all that is gone I find it impossible to understand these people who are unready in these days of national emergency to stabd up for the privileges and rights we have won for ourselves......For myself the path of duty was clear. This civilization of ours - built on ordered freedom and reason - must be upheld by every just and right means....16

Clynes was ultimately a democratic socialist and patriot, not an internationalist or an ideologue, whose ethical socialism led him to believe in the inherent good sense of his fellow citizens of all classes, and their capacity to respond to reasoned argument. This was essentially rooted in his understanding and experience of the native British people, and what he saw as their basic decency and good sense. The function of a democratic socialist party was to convince them of its principles and policies, and imbue them with a sense of what it means to be a human being being, sharing the same space and breathing the same air as others in equity and good fellowship.

NOTES

1. Introduction

1. Phil Woolas, 'J.R. Clynes' in Francis Beckett ed. *The Best Prime Ministers We Never Had: A Collection of Counter-Factuals* (2012)
2. J.R.Clynes, *Memoirs vol 2* (1937) p.294
3. The General Workers Union Journal Nov-Dec 1922 p.4

2. Young 'Piecer' Clynes

1. J. Foster, *Class Struggle and the Industrial Revolution: Early Industrial Competition in Three English Towns* (1974)
2. see D. Furr & J. Hunt, *The Cotton Mills of Oldham* (1998)
3. J.R. Clynes, *Memoirs vol. 1 1869-1924* (1937) pp. 29-30
4. ibid p. 31
5. ibid p. 32
6. Robert Roberts, *The Cassic Slum* (1990) pp.177-179
7. Jonathan Rose, *The Intellectual Life of the English Working Class* (2001) p.123
8. Clynes p.35
9. ibid p. 42
10. Edward George, *From Mill boy to Minister* p.28-29
11. Clynes p.33
12. ibid p. 44
13. Alan Fowler, *Lancashire Cotton Operatives and Work 1900-1950* (2007) p.15
14. Clynes p.14-15
15. ibid
16. Paul Morley, *The North: And Almost Everything in It* (p.201
17. ibid p.50-51
18. John Lauren ed., *Tom Mann's social and economic writing: a pre-syndicalist selection*

3. A Sixpenny Cigar

1. J.R. Clynes, *Memoirs vol. 1 1869-1924* (1937) p.56-57
2. ibid p. 64
3. ibid p.64
4. ibid p.69
5. E.A & G.H Radice, *Will Thorne: Constructive Militant* (1974) p55
6. Clynes, p.78
7. ibid p.79
8. ibid
9. Gas Worker's Union Quarterly Balance Sheet, March 1903
10. Richard Stevens, *Bolton Trades Council 187-1968* Microfilm Academic Publishing (1999) p. 2
11. Robert Taylor, 'John Robert Clynes and the Making of Labour Socialism, 1890-1918' in Matthew Worley ed. *The Foundation of the British Labour Party: Identities, Culture and Perspectives 1900-1939* (2009) p.22
12. Henry George, *From Mill Boy to Minister* (1917) p.52-53
13. Letter from Clynes to Keir Hardie 17 Nov. 1905 ILP Archive 190/154
14. Gasworkers Biennial Congress 1904
15. E.A. Radice & G.H. Radice, *Will Thorne: Constructive Militant* p.58

4. At Least a Party

1. Edward George, From Mill Boy to Minister (1917) pp. 57-58
2. Tony Lloyd 'J.R. Clynes' in Howarth & Hayter, *Men Who Made Labour* (2007) p.22
3. ibid p.28
4. J.R. Clynes, *Memoirs* (1937) p.110
5. ibid p. 115
6. George p. 66
7. *The Clarion* 26 Jan. 1906
8. David Clark, *Labour's Lost Leader: Victor Grayson* (1985) p.46
9. Clynes p. 120
10 HC Deb 30 May 1906 vol. 158 cc485-494
11. ibid 22 Nov. 1906 vol. 165 c969; 28 Nov. 1906 vol. 166 c33-4

12. Annual Report of Labour Party Conference 1909
13. Organisation of Labour Trades Councils Annual Report 1910 p.9
14. HC Deb 18 March 1908 vol. 186
15. ibid
16. Clynes p.128
17. Annual Report of Labour Party Conference 1908
18. Clynes p.129
19. ibid p.130
20. ibid p.132
21. Pugh, *Speak for Britain: A New History of the Labour Party* p.79
22. Patrick Yeates, 'Dublin Lockout 1913' *History Ireland* 9 (2)
23. GGLU Quarterly Bulletin Mar. 1913
24. E.A. Radice & G.H. Radice, *Will Thorne: Constructive Militant* (1974) p.89

5. War Years

1. Labour NEC Minutes, 5 Aug 1914; J.R. Clynes *Memoirs* (1937) p.172
2. Clynes, p.186
3. ibid p.190
4. Barbara Tizard, *Home is Where One Starts From: One Woman's Memoir* (2010) p.17
5. Clynes, p. 195-196
6. Gas and General Workers General Council Minutes, Nov. 1916
7. ibid p.187
8. E.A. Radice & G.H. Radice, *Will Thorne: Constructive Militant* (1974) p.74-77
9. ibid, p.90
10. E.A Turner, *Dear Old Blighty* p. (1982)
11. ibid p.78
12. Martin Pugh, *Speak for Britain: A New History of the Labour Party* (2009) p.119-120
13. B. Millman, *Managing Dissent in the First World War* (2000) p.167
14. A. Gregory, *The Last Great War* (2008) p.196
15. Clynes, p. 216

16. ibid p. 217
17. ibid p.219
18. ibid p. 237
19. John Grieve Smith, *There is a Better Way: A New Agenda for Labour* (2004) p. 6
20. Clynes p.243
21. Ian. F.W. Beckett, *The Home Front 1914-1918; How Britain Survived the Great War (*2006) p.380-182
22. Clynes p.245
23. Margaret Willes, *The Gardens of the Working Class* (2014) p.266
24. Clynes, p.113-114
25. ibid, p.254
26. ibid
27. Ian Gazely & Andrew Newell, 'The First World War and Working Class Food Consumption in Britain.' *English Review of Economic History* (2013) 17 (1) pp. 71-94
28. Clynes, p. 256
29. ibid p. 256
30. ibid, p.257
31. ibid

6. Breaking Through

1. J.C. Clynes, *Memoirs* vol 1 *1869-1924* (1937) p. 257
2. ibid p.230
3. ibid, 7 Jan 1919
4. ibid
5. Adam R. Seipp, *The Ordeal of Peace: Demobilization and the Urban Experience in Britain and Germany* 1917-1921 (2009) p.47-55
6. Clynes p. 298
7. ibid p. 318
8. Richard Hyman, *The Workers Union* (1974) Ch. V
9. General Worker's Union Biennial Conference 1920
10 Hyman Ch. V
11. HC Deb. 15 April 1921
12. Clynes p.252
13. ibid p. 325
14. David Kirkwood, *My Life in Revolt* (1935) p. 102
15.see Nicholas Owen, 'MacDonald's Parties: The Labour Party

15. see Nicholas Owen, 'MacDonald's Parties: The Lbaour Party and the Aristocratic Embrace, 1922-31' *Twentieth Century Britain* 18 2007

16. Clynes p. 344

7   Labour Troubles

1. *Daily Herald,* 4 Jan. 1924
2. Clynes, *Memoirs vol 2 1924-1937* (1937)
3. ibid p. 23
4. ibid p. 25-26
5. ibid p.55
6. *The Times* 21 April 1930
7. Clynes p.54
8. Ramsay MacDonald's Diary 26 Sept 1924; 1 Oct 1924
9. Clynes p.61
10. ibid p.64
11. ibid
12. Barbara Tizard, *Home is Where One Starts From: One Woman's Memoir* (2010) p.21-22
13. Clynes p.71
14 GMWU *Journal* May-June 1926
15. E.A. Radice & G.H. Radice, *Will Thorne, Constructive   Militant* (1974) p.98
16. GMWU Congress 1926
17. Radice p.106
18. ibid
19. Clynes p. 104
20. ibid p.95

8. Hope and Disaster

1. David Rubinstein, *The Labour Party and British Society 1880-2005* (2006) p.61
2. J.R. Clynes, *Memoirs vol. 2 1924-1937* (1937) p.112

3. Andrew J. Williams, *Labour and Russia: The Attitude of the Labour Party to the USSR 1924-1934* (1984)
4. CAB 24/204/13 24 June 1929
5. see Hugh Moulton, *The Trial of William Henry Podmore* Famous Trials Series (1931)
6. Clynes pp.141-144
7. ibid p.152
8. ibid p.158
9. ibid p.178
10. ibid p.182
11. Ibid
12. Rubinestein pp.63-64
13. Clynes pp 196-197
14. E.A. Radice & G.H. Radice, *Will Thorne: Constructive Militant* (1974) p.112
15. Clynes pp. 199
16. Diaries of Hugh Dalton 28 Aug 1931
17. Clynes ibid p.200
18. David Marquand, *Ramsay MacDonald* (1977) p.134

9. In the Wilderness

1. David Rubenstein, *The Labour Party and British Society 1880-2005* (2006) p.81
2. Clynes, *Memoirs vol 2 1924-1937* (1937)
3. Robert Taylor, 'John Robert Clynes and the Making of Labour Socialism 1890-1918' in Matthew Worley ed. *The Foundation of the British Labour Party: Identities, Culture and Perspectives 1900-1939*
4. Martin Pugh, *Speak for Britain: A New History of the Labour Party* p.220
5. Clynes p.230
6. *Labour Magazine* Aug. 1930; Anthony Wright, *R.H. Tawney* p.viii (1987)
7. Labour Party Conference Report 1935
8. Anthony Wright, *R.H. Tawney* (1987) p.viii
9. Ben Pimlott, *Hugh Dalton* (1985) p.21

10. Leicester Mercury Nov. 14 1933

10. Recovery to Victory

1. Martin Pugh, *Speak for Britain* pp.245-6
2. HC Deb 16 Nov 1936 cc1369
3. Clynes, *Memoirs vol. 2*, p. 239
4. ibid
5. HC Deb 22 May 1940 col 361 cc 185-195
6. ibid 18 July 1940 vol. 363 cc 447-543
7. J.R. Clynes, *Food in Wartime* (1942)
8. HC Deb 3 Mar 1942 vol 378 cc 535-618
9. Martin Pugh, *Speak for England* pp.267-268
10. ibid 10 Dec. 1943 vol 395 cc 1260-349
11. David Butler & Donald Stokes, *Political Change in Britain* (1969) p.77
12. Clynes p.204
13. *The Times* 16 June 1947
14. *The Spectator* 19 June 1947
15. Clynes p.211
16. HC Deb 25 Oct 1949
17. J.R. Clynes, *What I Remember* (1940) p13

BIBLIOGRAPHY

Primary Sources

Cabinet Papers (National Archives)
George Lansbury Papers (BLPES)
Hansard Historical Record
Ramsay MacDonald Papers *(NA)*
J.H. Thomas Papers (Kent CRO)
Ben Tillett Papers (Labour History Archive Manchester)
National Union of Gas Workers & General Labourers Archive
(National Archives
   Kew)
Trade Union Congress Reports (University of Warwick)

Newspapers

The *Clarion; New Leader; The Times, Spectator; Daily Mail; Daily Herald; New Statesman*

Secondary Sources

David Bilton, *The Home Front in the Great War*
Gregory Blaxland, *J.H. Thomas: A Life for Unity* (1964)
Neil Blewitt, *The Peers, the Party and the People: The General Elections of 1910* (1972)
Kenneth D. Brown, *Labour and Unemployment 1900-1914* (1971); *The First Labour Party 1906-1914* (1985)
John Callaghan, *Socialism in Britain since 1884* (1990); 'British Labour and Socialism in 1931' *Journal of Political Ideologies* vol 14 Issue 2 2009
Martin Ceadel, *Pacifism in Britain 1914-1945* (1980)
David Clarke, *Colne Valley, Radicalism to Socialism* (1981)
H.A. Clegg, *General Union : A Study of the NUGMW* (1954)
James E. Cronin, *New Labour's Pasts* (2004)
David Clarke, *Labour's Lost Leader: Victor Grayson* (1985)

J.R. Clynes, *Memoirs 1869-1924* vol 1(1937); *Memoirs 1924-1937 vol 2* (1937); *When I Remember (1940); Food in Wartime* (1941)

Alan Fowler, *Lancashire Cotton Operatives and Work 1900-1950* (2007); *The Barefoot Aristocrats: A History of the Amalgamated Society of Cotton Spinners* (1987)

A.J. Davies, *To Build a New Jerusalem: The Labour Movement from the 1880s to the 1990s* (1992)

Edward George, *From Mill Boy to Minister* (1918)

Reg Groves, *The Strange Case of Victor Grayson* (1975)

Trevor Griffiths, *The Lancashire Working Classes* 1880-1930 (2001)

Alan Howarth and Dianne Hayter, *Men Who Made Labour* (2007)

James Hinton, *Labour and Socialism: A History of the British Labour Movement 1867-1974* (1983)

David Howell, *British Workers and the Independent Labour Party 1888-1906* (1983); *MacDonald's Party: Labour Identity and Crisis 1922-1931* (2002)

Tony Judge, *Tory Socialist: Robert Blatchford and Merrie England* (2012)

Patrick Kyba, *Conflict without the Sword: Public: Opinion and British Disarmament Policy 1931-35* (1983)

William Lazonick, *Comparative Advantage on the Shop Floor* (1990)

David Marquand, *Ramsay MacDonald* (1977)

Ian McClean, *Keir Hardie* (1975)

Kenneth Morgan, *Keir Hardie, Radical and Socialist* (1975)

R.I. McKibbin, *The Evolution of the Labour Party 1910-1924* (1974)

Roger Moore, *The Emergence of the Labour Party 1880-1924* (1978)

Hugh Fletcher Moulton, *The Trial of William Henry Podmore* (1931)

Nicholas Owen, 'MacDonald's Parties: The Labour Party and the 'Aristocratic Embrace,' 1922-1931 *Twentieth Century Britain* 18 200

Anne Perkins, *A Very British Strike* (2006)

G.A. Phillips, *The General Strike* (1976)

Ben Pimlott, *Labour and the Left in the 1930's; Hugh Dalton* (1985)

David Powell, British Politics and the Labour Question *1868-1990* (1992)

Martin Pugh, *Speak for Britain: A New History of the Labour Party* (2010); *The Making of Modern British Politics 1867-1945* (2002); *The Pankhursts* (2000) 'The Rise of Labour and the Political Culture of Conservatism 1890-1945 *History'* 87, 288, 2002

E.A & G.H. Radice, Will Thorne: Constructive Militant (1974)

Fred Reid, *Keir Hardie, The Making of a Socialist* (1978)

Patrick Renshaw, *The General Strike* (1975)

Neil Riddell: *Labour in Crisis: The Second Labour Government 1929-31* (1999)

Jonathan Rose, *The Intellectual Life of the English Working Class* (2001)

David Rubinstein,*The Labour Party and British Society 1880-2005* (2006); Michael Savage, *The Dynamics of Working Class Politics: The Labour Movement in Preston, 1880-1940* (1967)

Caroline Seymour-Jones, *Beatrice Webb* (1992)

John Shepherd & Keith Laybourne, *Britain's First Labour Government* (2006)

J. Shepherd, J. Davis, C. Wrigley: *The Second Labour Government: A Reappraisal* (2012)

Jonathan Schneer, *Ben Tillett* (1982)

Robert Skidelsky, *Politicians and the Slump: the Labour government 1929-31* (1967)

Adrian Smith ed., *New Statesman: Portrait of a Political Weekly 1913-1931* (1996)

John Swift, *Labour in Crisis: Clement Attlee and the Labour Party in Opposition 1931-1940* (2001)

Jonathan Rose, *The Intellectual Life of the English Working Class* (2010)

Adam R. Seipp, *The Ordeal of Peace: Demobilization and the Urban Experience in Britain and Germany 1918-1921* (2009)

R. Swift & S. Gilley (eds), *The Irish in Britain 1815-1939* (1989)

Daniel Tanner, *Political Change and the Labour Party 1900-1918* (1990)

Laurence Thompson, *The Enthusiasts, A Biography of Bruce and Katherine Bruce Glasier* (1971)

Will Thorne, *My Life's Battles* (1926)

Richard Toye. *The Labour Party and the Planned Economy 1931-51* (2003); 'Perfectly Parliamentary'? The Labour Party and the House of Commons in the Inter-war Years' *Twentieth Century History* vol. 24, No 1, 2014 pp.1-29

Paul Ward, *Red Flag and Union Jack: Englishness, Patriotism and the British Left 1881-1914* (1998)

Matthew Worley, *Inside the Gate: A History of the British Labour Party between the Wars* (2005); ed. *The Foundation of the British Labour Party: Identity, Culture and Perspectives 1900-1939* (2009)

Chris Wrigley, *Arthur Henderson* (1990)

INDEX